THE PROBLEM HORSE & THE PROBLEM HORSEMAN

MARGARET CABELL SELF

Illustrated by Diana Butler

ARCO PUBLISHING COMPANY, INC.
NEW YORK

Published by Arco Publishing Company, Inc.
219 Park Avenue South, New York, N.Y. 10003

Copyright © 1977 by Margaret Cabell Self

All rights reserved. No portion of this book may be reproduced in any form or by any means without permission in writing from the publisher, except by a reviewer.

Library of Congress Cataloging in Publication Data

Self, Margaret Cabell.
   The problem horse and the problem horseman.

   1. Horse-training. 2. Horsemanship. 3. Horses—Behavior
I. Title.

SF287.S42   636.1'08'8   75-38952
ISBN 0-668-03934-5

Printed in the United States of America

Contents

I	**What Constitutes a Problem Horse?**	5
	Underlying Causes Which Result in a "Problem" Horse	6
II	**Reactions of Various Types of Horses to Rough Treatment and Suggested Methods of Overcoming the Resulting Resistance**	11
	The Timid Horse	11
	The Aggressive Horse	18
	The Sulky or Stubborn Horse	31
III	**Problems Arising From Confusion**	37
	Confusion Due to Bad Training	62
	Training the Young or the Problem Jumper	67
	The Horse That Has Been Bred and Trained for Racing	73
IV	**Everyday Problems to Be Expected When Working With Young or Partially Trained Horses**	78
	Shying	78
	Bolting	82

	The Barn-Rat or Herd Bound Horse	84
	Rearing	86
	The Balky Horse	89
	Bucking	90
	The Horse That Attempts to Brush the Rider Off or Crowd Him Against a Wall or Fence	90
	Restlessness While Being Mounted	91
	Stall Courage	95
	Rolling in the Saddle	98
	Tossing the Head	98
	Above the Bit	98
	Bits and Bitting	99
	Bitting	104
	Problems in the Stable	105
	Crowding in the Stall	105
	Kicking the Side of the Stall	106
	Cribbing and Sucking Wind	106
	Halter Breaking and Leading	109
	Problems With Clipping	111
	Vanning	114
	Controlling the Nervous Horse for Medication	118
	Catching the Horse in the Field	118
V	**The Problem Horseman**	120
	What Constitutes a Problem Horseman?	120
	What Leads to the Development of a Problem Rider?	121
	The Horse as Instructor	122
	The Timid Rider	122
	The Over-Bold Rider	123
	The Horseman's Goal	123
	Developing the Ability to Feel	125
	Upper Body Position	132
	The Rider's Hands	134
	Learning to Interpret	137
	Learning to Influence	139
	Index	142

I
What Constitutes a Problem Horse?

At some point in his training every horse presents one kind of problem or another. This is because, like humans, horses are individuals with specific aptitudes and disabilities. Teaching them movements and exercises which are difficult for them to learn always challenges the rider's or trainer's skill, knowledge, and ingenuity.

Horses which present only these to-be-expected resistances to learning are not really "problem" horses, since under careful schooling these resistances quickly disappear. Horses which have exaggerated reactions of one kind or another to ordinary demands are something else again. These are what one would call "problem" horses, in the pathological sense.

This book will deal with various methods of controlling and reschooling the spoiled horse as well as methods of handling normal problems which come up during the training of most young horses. Some of these methods have been used by trainers over the centuries. Some are ones which I have found useful in encountering horses which do not respond to those commonly used. The wise horseman keeps an open mind, and when one method doesn't work he patiently continues until he finds one that will.

UNDERLYING CAUSES WHICH RESULT IN A "PROBLEM" HORSE

There are several underlying causes which turn a horse which would normally be a willing and obedient companion into a disobedient and occasionally dangerous creature. The first of these is FEAR.

Yet, had Eohippus (also known as the "dawn horse," the original ancestor of horses as we know them today) not been a highly fearful creature, his species would never have survived, because he had no method of defense other than running away from his enemies. Eohippus was born with such long legs and light weight that a few hours after birth he could keep up with the galloping herd. He was endowed with special, sling-like joints in his legs which enabled him to sleep standing up and so be ready to take off at the slightest rustle of leaves or scent of danger. It is this "excitement to flight" imprinted 50,000,000 years ago which makes the horse valuable to man, but with it goes a nervous system which can make him difficult to handle and easily spoiled.

Fear is related in the horse's mind to unhappy or painful experiences. The highly bred, hot-blooded horse with his thin skin is particularly susceptible. Under rough or cruel treatment he may develop a pathological fear of mankind as a whole. This can make him dangerous either to handle or to approach. This will rarely happen, however. More likely he will simply become so timid that only an exceedingly sensitive horseman can manage him.

The colder-blooded, thicker-skinned horse may adjust to such treatment although he, too, can become an outlaw if pushed too far. In any case, although he may have been taught to submit to domination by violence, when he really becomes frightened he will have no confidence in his rider and hence can be even more dangerous than the nervous horse who has learned to depend on his trainer.

Fear can also be generated in the horse through the ignorance, inexperience, and lack of skill of the rider. It is the highly trained, alert, and supersensitive animal which suffers most from this type of fear. Brought along slowly and ridden only by

The third cause of pathological fear is fear of a specific thing. In this case a rabbit.

Confusion caused by the misuse of the aids may result in a normally well-mannered animal planting his rider rather unexpectedly.

those who know what they are doing, an excitable Thoroughbred, American Saddlebred, or Arabian will develop into the best of mounts. His rider will have only to think and he will obey instantly. Subjected to heavy, rough hands and a too-severe use of the legs or spurs, he may become an outlaw through fear and even get the reputation of being a "man-killer."

A third cause of pathological fear is some specific *thing*. This is usually the result of an unforeseen incident or happening, probably occurring in colthood. This is not as dangerous as the general fear of being hurt, but it can be very difficult to overcome.

The second underlying cause which results in the development of problem horses is CONFUSION. The well-trained horse has been taught to obey a certain language: the language of the aids. When he obeys, the tension of rein or leg or the use of the rider's back and weight is relaxed. This constitutes his reward for obeying. If an ignorant rider who does not understand these principles tries to ride such an animal, the result is chaos. Not understanding the feeling of heavy hands which do not yield when he obeys, of squeezing legs, even, perhaps of punishing spurs, or of the uneasy shifting of the loose seat, the sensitive horse soon becomes resistant and then frantic. At this stage he may not intend to unseat the rider, but frequently he does. If the punishment continues the horse will become more and more unmanageable and develop some defensive vice such as rearing or plunging. The confusion in his mind, resulting from having been conditioned to one type of treatment only to receive another, brings on what in a human being would be called a "nervous breakdown."

Under these conditions, a well-trained but less nervous animal may react differently. Annoyed rather than frightened, he may take to bolting, bucking, or rearing with the idea of getting rid of the tormentor on his back. If he succeeds in doing so more than a couple of times, a habit which may easily develop into a vice will have been set up. This horse, too, will become a pathological problem animal.

Sometimes a young horse, being trained by a well-meaning and kind but over-eager rider, will become resistant and unmanageable because his training has been rushed. Things are demanded of him which he is not yet ready to learn. The results can be similar to those described above. If he does not go to such extremes, the horse will react by being stiff and uncomfortable in his gaits and by having a bad head carriage. There are many variations of the latter which will be taken up later, but they all show a desire to escape the bit instead of accepting it and yielding to it.

Another underlying cause of problems which may develop into vices is that of HIGH SPIRITS plus LACK OF EXERCISE and too much GRAIN. A rider with moderate experience buys a young horse in the summer season. He gives him regular work as long as the good weather lasts. Then comes winter with its cold, its wind, and its bad footing due to ice or snow. Our young horse stands in his stall day after day or, at best, is turned into a small paddock while the stall is being cleaned. Meanwhile he is being fed his normal ration of hard grain. Finally there comes a brisk, bright, sparkling day. The footing is now good and the owner is delighted to get out on the trail again. He hurries into his togs and prepares to climb aboard. But the docile, obedient animal to which he is accustomed has suddenly developed all sorts of habits that he never exhibited before. He will hardly stand still to be mounted. He dances all over the paddock while the rider tries to settle himself in the saddle. On the road he shies at every excuse and may even put in a high-spirited buck or two. In a word, the descendant of Eohippus has suddenly developed his "winter disposition." All his senses are keyed up and he is ready to see a sabretoothed tiger behind every bush.

In the following chapters we will discuss the handling of the various types of resistance resulting from the causes listed above. It must be emphasized that in no case is the horse to blame when he develops such undesirable habits. Also, given experience and patience, no matter how difficult or dangerous the animal may appear to be, he can usually be reschooled successfully and will become a useful and enjoyable mount PROVIDED he is thenceforth ridden by a person capable of riding him as he should be ridden.

II

Reactions of Various Types of Horses to Rough Treatment and Suggested Methods of Overcoming the Resulting Resistance

THE TIMID HORSE

The immediate reaction of the timid horse to rough treatment is fear of mankind. This horse will be difficult to approach either in the field or in his stall, especially when he is in the latter, as fear of being unable to escape will be added to his fear of attack. He will be nervous and tense even when there is no reason to be so. He will be difficult to handle for medication, shoeing, clipping, or when something unusual is expected of him. When he is approached while eating he will stop eating and raise his head, holding the grain in his mouth without swallowing. In extreme cases he may begin to tremble and will always tend to flinch from an extended hand instead of nuzzling it in hopes of a treat. In other words, he will have the attitude of a child that has been abused and fears further punishment. Any knowledgeable horseman can tell on entering a stable whether the horses in it are handled roughly or with kindness.

Since the first object of training is to have the horse relaxed, unafraid, and cooperative, the trainer, rider, or stableman who starts by making his charge afraid of him will never attain this goal. The horse should respect the master but never be in abject fear of a sudden blow. If the brutal treatment becomes too severe even the timid horse, like the cornered rat, may some day be goaded to active defense methods.

Reschooling a timid animal that has had one or more bad experiences and persuading him to have confidence in mankind is one of the most difficult problems to be encountered. Often, after many hours, weeks, or even months of careful, kind treatment we may feel that he is cured of his fears and that his confidence in us is established. Then, some sudden happening—the abrupt raising of a hand near his head, the entanglement in a rope, the slamming of a gate in his face—may drive him into a panic and he may let fly with both heels. With such a horse, the wise horseman never places himself in a vulnerable position and is forever watchful to avoid similar situations.

However, much can be accomplished. One must begin as though this horse had never been subjected to any kind of handling, for his fears are usually associated with something that has been done to him by a man on foot. He must be treated as one treats a young foal. This means getting him accustomed to grooming, to having his feet lifted and picked out, and to being handled and stroked all over his body and head.

In working around the timid horse, it is best to have him cross-tied in a wide aisle. Never work on him when he is loose in a box stall. Should you make an unexpected move or should he become frightened for some other reason, he might swing his quarters and pin you into a corner where you would be defenseless.

With your horse cross-tied you start your grooming and rubbing on the body and upper legs, later moving up the neck. If he is very headshy, it may be some time before he will consent to lower his head and let you rub his poll. In extreme cases he will never come to really enjoy this. A helper standing nearby and offering an occasional tidbit or holding a shallow pan with oats in it from which he can nibble will help him to become relaxed.

Many horses, especially those shipped in from the West, which are not used to having their feet cleaned every day, or horses from Mexico, which are sometimes shod by force before they know what it is all about, may give trouble when it comes to picking up their feet. Go about the whole matter quietly. Stroke the horse's shoulder and upper left leg, gradually continuing

Next lean your own shoulder against that of the horse and lift the foot, bending the fetlock joint and cupping the hoof in your hand.

down to the foot. Next lean your own shoulder against that of the horse and lift the foot, bending the fetlock joint and cupping the hoof in your hand. Hold it only an instant if the horse is restless, then put it down gently and reward the animal with a bit of carrot. If he tries to pull away, do your best to hold on so that it will be you and not the horse who decides when the foot is to be released. Try, however, not to make it into a fighting affair, and if he is too nervous, be content with just stroking the pastern and rubbing the wall without lifting it from the ground.

Wait until he is relaxed about his front feet before attempting to lift his hind feet. It often takes much longer for the horse to permit his hind feet to be handled.

If, before you have had your timid horse long enough to gain his confidence, it becomes necessary to shoe him or to give him medical treatment, you will have to resort to the use of the twitch.

Contrary to what many people believe, the twitch is not an instrument of torture provided it is used on the upper lip (or on the lower if it is the upper lip that must be treated) and never on the ear. The instrument itself is made of a smooth stick with a rounded end and cord (and it should be a cord, never a chain) of soft cotton. Twelve or fourteen inches cut from the top of a broom or rake handle makes an excellent twitch. Get a blacksmith or veterinarian to show you how to put it on and be sure that you twist it tight enough to pinch the lip and distract the horse, but not tight enough to panic him. Strangely enough, the use of the twitch does not make a horse headshy in itself and as soon as it is removed he forgets it. However, I owned one horse that had been so brutally treated before I got him that I never attempted to use a twitch on him. Fortunately, in the eighteen years that we had him he never had to be medically treated or have his teeth floated, and since he was only afraid of being handled around his head, never around his feet, shoeing did not present a problem.

This horse, Sky Rocket, about whom I once wrote a book,* was only one of a number of horses which came into my stable with a terrible fear concerning bridling and general handling of

---

* *Sky Rocket, The Story of a Little Bay Horse* (Dodd Mead).

his head. Another was one whom we called Mr. X, the reason being that the dealer, who sold him to me very cheaply, had promised never to reveal his name. He was a magnificent animal, a registered Thoroughbred (though, of course, his papers did not go with him), six years old when I acquired him without a mark or a blemish and not a single bad habit or vice except this terrible headshyness. I was told that he had been a triple-bar jumper and had won many ribbons. Then, some groom, handler, rider, or trucker had frightened him, probably by clubbing him over the head. From that day on, he would permit no man to approach his head. It was impossible to get a bridle on him and he was said to have attacked and badly injured one or two men who tried.

I did not know his story the day I drove into the dealer's yard just to see if he had anything for sale that was good and cheap, for those were the Depression days and every penny counted. The first thing I saw was this lovely, lean chestnut head with a white blaze hanging out over the lower half of a box-stall door. The dealer himself, an old friend, was gone for the day but his stableman was there and the latter allowed that yes, the owner of the lovely head was for sale, and that he could jump. However, when I asked that he be tacked up, the man merely grunted something, indicated the tack, and disappeared into another part of the barn.

When I entered the stall carrying the saddle and with the bridle hung over my arm, the horse shied away and rolled his eyes until the whites showed. So I put the saddle on the top of the door and hung the bridle over my arm. Then I went up to the horse, patted his shoulder, and talked to him for a moment until he relaxed.

There is a certain method which is usually successful in bridling headshy horses. Instead of approaching from the front and standing on the left beside the horse's head, then slipping the bridle over the muzzle from the side and then slipping the crownpiece up to the ears, one stands well back at the shoulder. Now, holding one cheek piece in each hand about halfway down, bring the crownpiece and brow band up from below, slip it over the muzzle, carry it up a few inches, then grasp the two cheekpieces with the right hand and hold them together over the

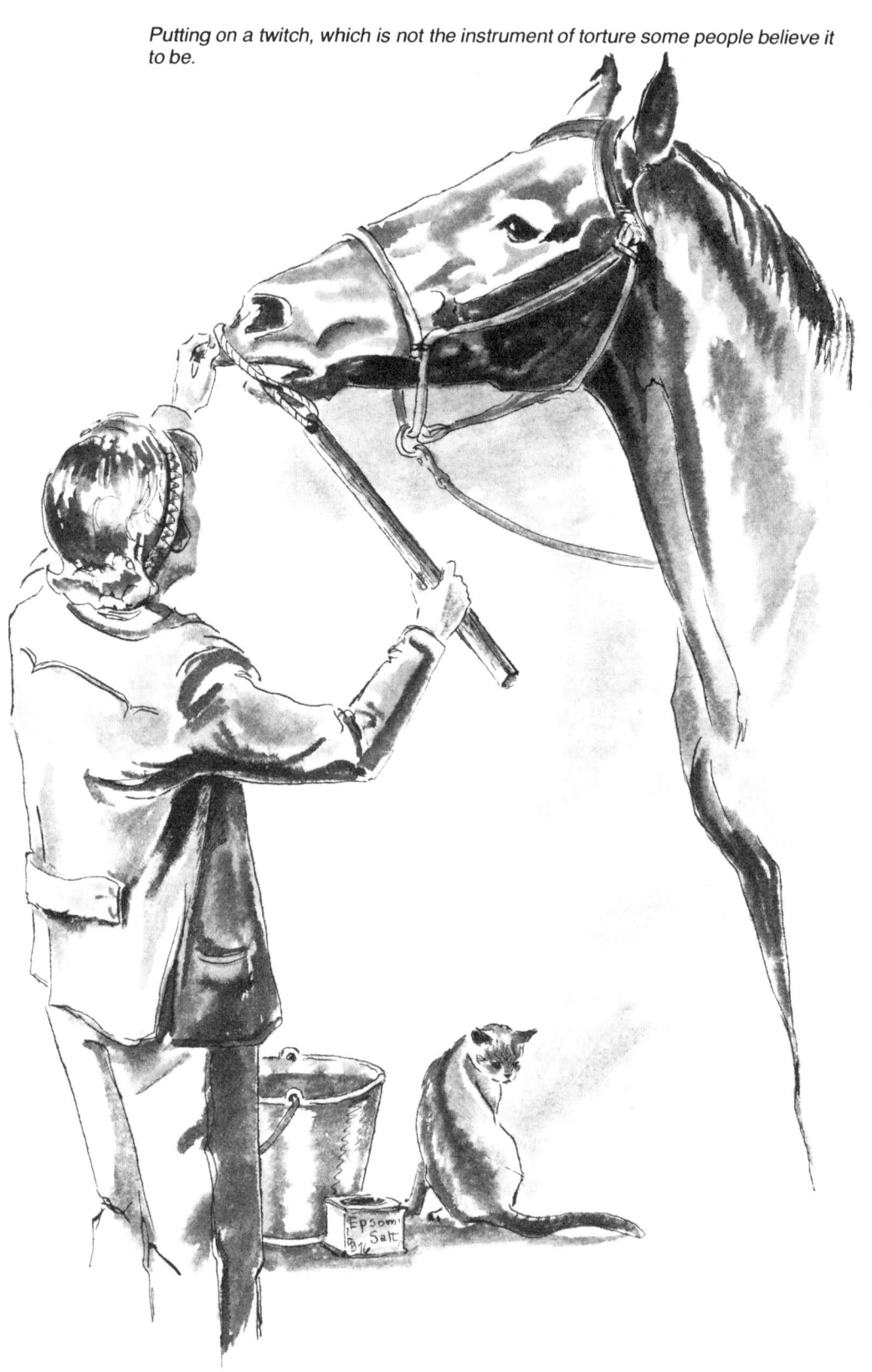
Putting on a twitch, which is not the instrument of torture some people believe it to be.

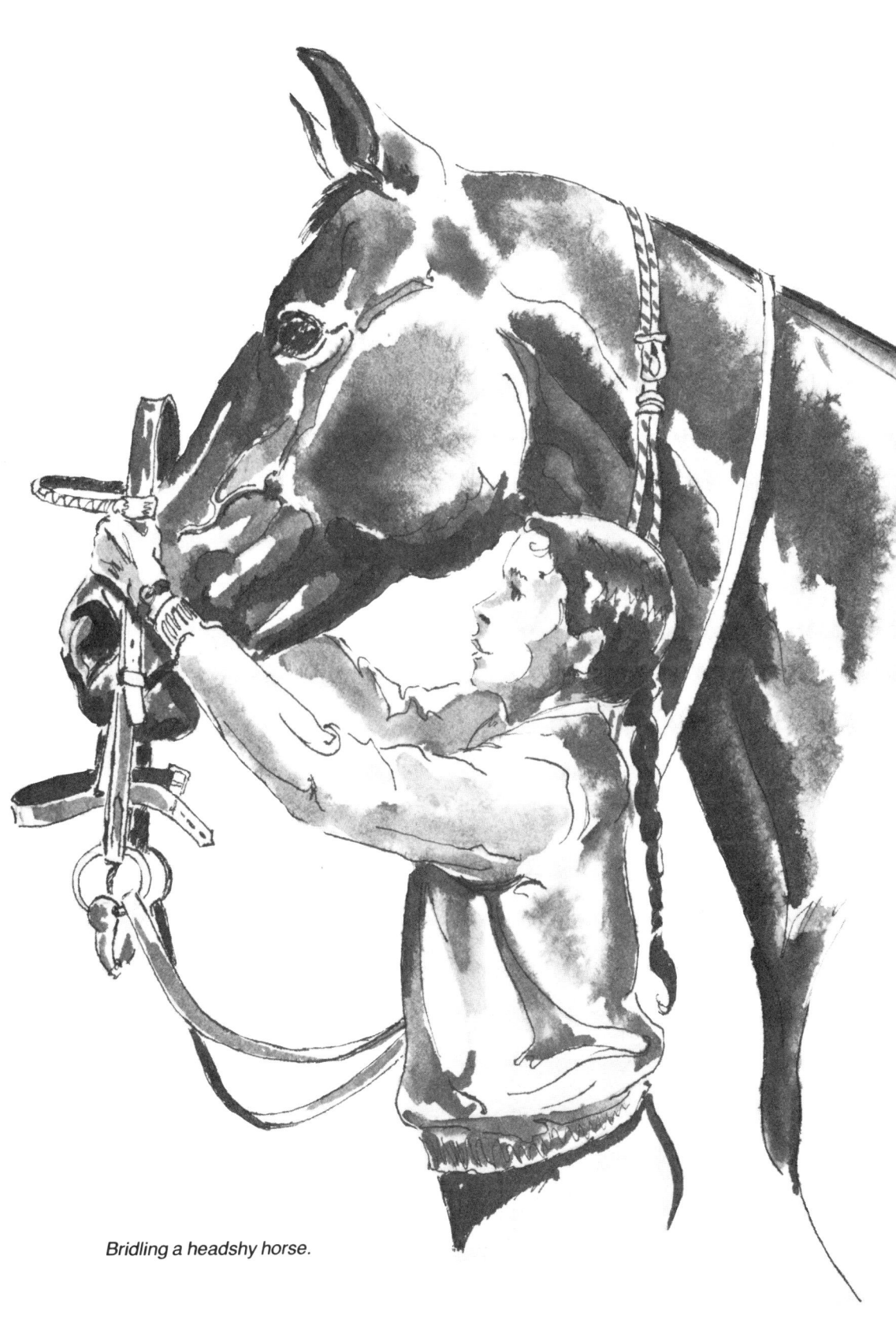
Bridling a headshy horse.

nose about opposite the cheek bones. Your arm should be under the horse's jaw. The left hand now cups the chin in the usual fashion, either the thumb or the fingers of that hand entering the mouth at the bars. This causes the horse to open his mouth, at which the right hand pulls the bridle up to the lips, the bit slips into his mouth and quietly, still working from below, the right hand slides the crownpiece and browband into place. The trick is never to bring either hand in front of the muzzle or head of the horse, since this is what he is afraid of.

Mr. X behaved perfectly normally as I bridled him using this procedure, and it was a surprised dealer who, on returning, saw me riding him in the schooling field.

I bought the horse for a song, but knew that I would have to get him over his fears if he was to be safe in the stable where two hundred youngsters were learning to handle, ride, and train horses.

For the first two weeks I allowed no one else to work in the stall with him or tack him up. My next step was to cross-tie him with his head over the open top half of his stall and door. The pupils were told that they might offer him tidbits and pat his nose every time they passed his stall but never to try to reach up toward his ears. Before long he was entirely over his headshyness and anyone could bridle him using the ordinary method. However, I realized that he was still nervous whenever one person held the reins and another person mounted, or when a hand or arm was suddenly raised near his head, and that he had never entirely forgotten the terrible experience that had given him the reputation of "man-killer," so I was always watchful to see that whoever rode him understood this fear.

THE AGGRESSIVE HORSE

Fortunately, the horse that becomes dangerously aggressive under rough treatment is not nearly so common as the one which responds by merely becoming more and more timid. However, as pointed out, the latter, if pushed too far, will become dangerous, but in a defensive way.

Aggressive horses are of two classes: those that are bad-tempered with their own kind and those that attack humans. Although there may be horses or ponies which are aggressive toward both other equines and their masters, I have yet to run across one. It is very possible that there are bloodlines or families of horses which are somewhat predisposed toward bad temper and aggressiveness, but I do not believe that the foal is born with either the instinct or the desire to attack. Nor do I believe that a foal accustomed to gentle handling and kind treatment from birth would ever be likely to develop true aggressiveness toward humans. If, having been carefully trained, he were later to fall into bad hands and undergo rough treatment, he might very well become excessively timid and manshy; he might even be aggressive if cornered. But I doubt if, loose in the field and with no provocation, he would deliberately charge a human being with the intent of savaging him with teeth or hooves.

Much has been said and is believed about the innate aggressiveness and bad temper of stallions. There are certainly many stallions which are not to be trusted and which must be handled with great care. But I refuse to believe that all stallions are dangerously unmanageable.

The basic reason behind this old wives' tale, which many consider an established fact, is that most people not acquainted with stallions are automatically afraid of them, and approach them on the offensive. The large majority of stallions are kept for breeding purposes only. They are not properly exercised by being ridden several hours a day, preferably in company. The stablemen or grooms who look after them never enter a stallion's stall without a pitchfork or other weapon which they wave at the poor prisoner if he tries to approach them. And the only time that this strong, lusty creature, which for centuries knew no barriers but roamed at will with his band of mares, is released from his cell of solitary confinement is when, in a state of excitement and anticipation, he is brought prancing forth to be introduced to a mare in heat.

Is there any reason to believe that males of any other species of animal would not react in the same way under the same conditions! What about a male dog kept continuously shut up alone, clubbed or at least threatened if he attempted to approach. Would he, too, not be somewhat unmanageable?

Personally I have had a great deal to do with stallions of many breeds: Thoroughbreds, American Saddlebreds, Morgans, Arabians, Shetlands, Welsh, Standardbreds, and crossbreds. One or two I have bought after they were adults and already trained to the saddle, but the majority I have either raised from birth or bought between the ages of two and four and broken and trained myself. I have handled them just as I would fillies or gelded colts. We consistently ride them in company both with each other and with mares and geldings. Children as young as eight or ten but who have light hands and are capable of riding a well-trained horse with spirit ride them in the ring, on trails, and in formation riding, and we never have any problems. We keep them stabled in stalls in which the upper four feet of all partitions is chain fence so that the stallion can have companionship and sniff noses with the animals on either side. We also use them for breeding, of course.

I once visited the ranch in Texas belonging to Mr. Rex Cauble. Mr. Cauble raised and trained cutting horses for competition. He had several hundred, including mares, foals, young stock, and four or five stallions. He, too, believed in using his stallions as working animals and they were ridden and worked in company. They were all quiet and mannerly, both to ride and to handle on foot, nor did they give any trouble when brought out for service.

A neighbor in Connecticut decided to go in for breeding Thoroughbreds with the idea of getting racing stock of recognized bloodlines and selling off the fillies and colts when they became yearlings. She brought a number of brood mares and one stallion. After buying the latter she was warned that he was a real "man-killer." And so he appeared to be when she first brought him home. She kept him in a field next to the house and started by putting an elderly mare of quiet disposition in with him for company. He was turned out day and night. Gradually she got him gentle enough to come up to her for a tidbit, then to allow himself to be tied to a post, handled all over and groomed. When I made his acquaintance a year or two later he was so gentle that the general practice when bringing the herd in from pasture to be fed was for the mares and foals to run ahead down the road which led from pasture to barn, while one person drove a jeep with one hand and led the stallion by a short rope with the other.

The erstwhile man-killing stallion is led home from the field to his stable.

When my friend Harold Black decided to start a riding school, *La Escuela Ecuestre*, in San Miguel Allende, he told me that he wanted to keep a stallion or so and raise some colts. I advised him to use his stallions as school horses as well. This he does, and they, like the ones I have worked with, are no more difficult to handle in company than any well-bred, spirited, well-trained, sensitive mare or gelding.

However, there are a few differences. The mare is actually more apt to be undependable, especially with other horses and mares, than is the stallion—especially when she is in heat. For this reason many dressage riders prefer stallions to mares. The mare defends herself by kicking. The stallion, and quite often the gelding, is more prone to attack by biting and occasionally rearing and striking. The reason for these differences is that when the prehistoric head was attacked by encircling wolves or other animals that ran in packs, it formed a compact mass. The mares stood on the outer edges with their heads to the center and haunches to the outside, ready to meet an onslaught, the foals and young stock were in the center of the circle, and the stallions circled around the perimeter, using teeth and front legs on the enemy. When mares fight, they back up to each other and kick and squeal. Stallions approach head on and each tries to grab the withers of his opponent with his teeth and force him to his knees. These things should be remembered in handling aggressive animals of either sex.

I have used the term "defensively aggressive" in regard to animals that have orginally been well-trained and well-treated and are therefore fundamentally friendly and reliable but which have met with cruel treatment later. These horses (or ponies) do not attack aggressively but will defend themselves by kicking if approached in a manner which reminds them of the former mistreatment. In dealing with them it is simply necessary to remember their history and never to allow such a situation to arise.

This was the case with our little Shetland stallion. He first made our acquaintance at the age of three when we arranged to have him shipped to Connecticut for breeding purposes. He came from the Belle Meade Farm in Virginia, the first of many very satisfactory ponies which we later bought and had sent North. He was ten hands two inches in height, a piebald, per-

Shoebutton, a pony stallion was so well-mannered that the children could climb all over him.

fectly trained to ride and so beautifully mannered that our five-year-old son could climb all over him, playing with him as though he were a dog and riding him either alone or in company. He came with the impressive stable name of Belle Meade Success, but from the first we called him "Shoebutton" because on his white rump there was a large black patch in the shape of a circle from the center of which extended his glorious white tail, for all the world as though someone had sewn a button, two feet in diameter, on his rump and allowed the thread to dangle.

We became so fond of him that we offered to buy him but were told that he was not for sale. So, at the end of a month, we sadly sent him back.

Two years later I received a letter from the owner of Belle Meade Farm, telling me that Shoebutton was now for sale and that at the moment he was in Mt. Kisco, a town not far from where we lived.

Of course we could hardly wait to see him, and with a generous supply of carrots the two oldest children and I set out. The stable to which we went was a magnificent affair with immaculately clean stalls glistening with varnish and highly polished brassware. A whole army of grooms seemed to be in attendance, rubbing away on shining withers and rumps, washing white legs, sweeping aisles and soaping leather. I wondered if we were doing a kindness in taking Shoey away from such luxury to our much simpler establishment.

When I asked one of the men about the little stallion and showed him Dr. Elliot's letter, he seemed somewhat surprised. Then he called an old stableman over and told him to take us to Shoey's quarters.

"I hope you wouldn't be letting the children come near the little devil," remarked the man morosely as he picked up a pitchfork and led us down a back path away from the main stable. "Sure it's only meself dares go near him and that only when I have a good weepon with me!"

I couldn't believe my ears! Shoebutton, dangerous? There must be some mistake. Perhaps Dr. Elliott had forgotten which stallion he had sent us.

The little shack to which we were led looked as though it had been intended only for storage. There were no windows and no light or ventilation except through the air spaces between the rafters where the walls joined the roof, for the door was obviously kept shut all the time.

The man slid the bolt and opened the door. We saw a little black and white shape which immediately took refuge in a far corner, cringing and presenting its hindquarters to us. Yes, it was Shoebutton. Without question it was Shoebutton, although I should never have recognized him had it not been for that peculiar marking on his rump. His coat was dull, and although it was now July he had not shed out. From the hipline down he was matted with manure and even through the dirt and the heavy coat you could see his ribs. His eyes were dull—those of a creature that has lost all hope.

"Get over there before I lam you one," said the man, waving the pitchfork, and the poor little fellow, tucking his tail tightly into his buttocks, tried to squeeze himself even more snugly into the corner.

We sent back for him that same afternoon. It took much quiet handling, talking, and rewarding with bits of carrots to restore Shoey's faith in the human race. Nor did he ever entirely get over the effects of his terrible experiences in Mt. Kisco. He was gentle to groom and ride, but let anyone try and corner him or wave a stick at him from behind and he tucked in his tail ready to let fly.

Skip, the boy who had ridden him before, did not realize this at first and tried to catch him by herding him into a corner of the paddock. Before I could shout to him he got within range and received a kick which gave him a scar he will bear forever. But this was the only time that Shoey ever harmed anyone and it was not his fault for the reaction was completely automatic, beaten into his very soul by the mistreatment.

He lived to the age of thirty-two and was passed down the family to each child as the older ones outgrew him. He served in the riding school under all kinds of riders, was hunted and shown, and even at thirty-two was still as sound as the proverbial dollar. However, he had worn his teeth away until he could no longer chew either hay or hard grain and he would not eat soft food. So, reluctantly, we had to put the old fellow down. I miss him to this day. I think the factor that proves that aggressiveness was foreign to Shoey's nature, but rather a result of being conditioned to resort to it through fear, is that he never, in his long life, attacked a human being by charging or biting, the stallion's natural method of attack. He only used the defensive action of his heels that one time, when put into the same situation that had given him this terrible fear of being cornered with no way of escape from what he thought was the threat of brutal attack.

Let us now consider the best methods of handling horses that have become dangerously aggressive towards man. The first rule is to study the type of attack used by that particular horse and the situations which lead up to it, and then never place yourself in a vulnerable position.

Next, one must decide on what has caused or is causing this reaction. For example, many colts, geldings, and young horses bite. This is particularly true of ponies. With the latter, the cause is generally that of too much feeding of tidbits from the hand. Every time the owner approaches the animal expects a treat. He starts by nudging to express his desires, then may nip a few times and finally may come to giving a sharp bite. From this some horses develop a biting complex whenever approached, even though normally they are not getting tidbits.

If it has been decided that the animal is biting for the reason given above, the first thing to do is to stop all hand-feeding. When the horse has finished work he should be put into his stall and a few carrots should be placed in his manger or feed box. Instead of rewarding him with carrots while working, give him a pat on the shoulder, a word of praise, and let him walk on a long rein.

This is not to say that every horse will necessarily become a biter as a result of being fed from the hand. Many will not, and as long as they show no signs of becoming biters, a tidbit before starting and after finishing work, and perhaps immediately after the performance of a difficult movement, is all right. Ponies, being very subject to this vice, should not be so rewarded.

Another piece of advice is to be careful at all times when working abound the head and shoulders of a known biter. The instant the ears go back and the peculiar snakelike attitude of the head is noticed, a sharp word and a sharp slap on the muzzle will usually prevent the attack. Follow this with a caress around the

A sharp word and a slap given the instant the attitude of the horse shows that he is preparing to bite will usually prevent his doing so.

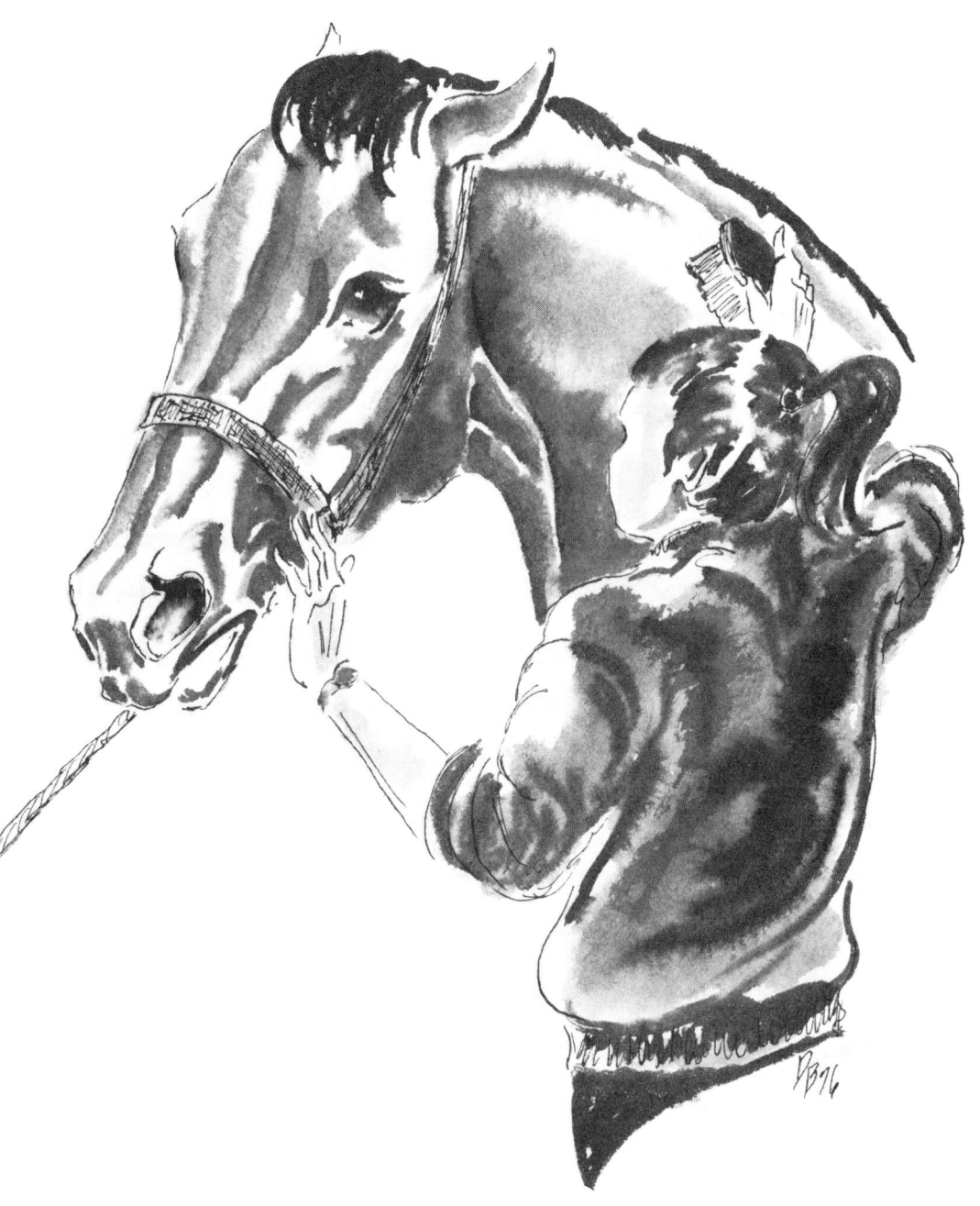

head to show that the horse has received his punishment and now all is forgiven. Never jump back, but meet the aggression with punishment. You should not anticipate the bad action, but be sure that you are ready if it should occur.

Another cause for the development of the biting habit, especially in young stallions and geldings, can be not having any playmates while growing up. A couple of weanlings, yearlings, or two-year-olds will spend hours having mock battles and lightly nipping each other in the pasture. They are in the process of shedding their baby teeth and their gums itch. They long to bite something. Furthermore in this fashion they also work out their natural instinct to preserve a certain amount of space or personal territory around themselves as individuals.

Occasionally a young horse will be restive while being groomed and will tend to reach around and nip gently at his attendant. I have found that giving such a horse a rubber curry comb to bite on and play with is often very helpful and will prevent him from starting a bad habit.

We come now to the compulsive biter. This is usually a gelding and often one which has not been correctly castrated. These animals will usually readily learn to respect a horseman who is ready for them if they attack but they will never be safe with strangers or timid riders. If there is danger of their being approached by an unknowledgeable person, the best thing to do is to keep them muzzled while working or being worked around. Generally speaking, this will be their only fault. One of the most satisfactory ponies regarding obedience under the saddle and calmness and willingness even when ridden by a very unskillful beginner was a pony named Scooter. He was a compulsive biter when we got him. He gave no trouble either in the field or in the stall when approached or handled by someone he knew, but he would attack a strange child or adult. We never cured him but we were always careful to put a leather muzzle on him before the riders came to ride and to let only an experienced person tack or untack him.

There are horses that are not compulsive biters but that have developed the habit of charging in the pasture in order to escape being caught. They can usually be broken of this by a bold horseman who stands ready with a stout stick and gives the charging animal a sharp blow on the nose just as he gets within biting distance. The horseman must be alert, however, for some horses charge as though they were going to attack with their teeth, then, at the last moment, whirl and let fly with their heels.

Here again one must change the situation. Never go into the pasture with such a horse to catch him. He should preferably be turned out into a paddock adjoining his stall where feed can be put into the manger and the horse allowed to enter by himself. If it is necessary to come up to him in the stall, and he is in a box stall with a half door, open the top half, coax the horse to come up to you by holding out a handful of grass or rattling oats in a bucket, and take hold of his halter before you go into the stall with him. If you must catch him in the pasture, leave a two-foot halter shank attached to his halter at all times. Go up to the gate or drawbars and get the horse to come up to you, reaching forward not for his head but for the dangling rope.

The horse that kicks at human beings, not to defend himself but whenever he thinks he can get away with it, may have been a perfectly nice animal to start with. Then he must have been either very cruelly treated or handled in a way which frightened him. This horse is truly dangerous unless he is handled entirely by one person whom he respects but does not fear. If there is any chance that inexperienced people may put themselves in danger it would be best to get rid of him. However, I must say again that sometimes a horse that seems incurable can be rehabilitated and will get back his confidence in humans over a period of time.

Curing the horse that is aggressive toward his companions while being ridden is comparatively easy, since this is not an instinctive behavior pattern. It is true that when a newcomer is introduced to a herd that has been running together for some time he will be chased around for several days. This goes back to the ancient, instinctive behavior patterns which have come down to the present. It was important to the wild horses that the size of the herd be limited. Usually there was a mature stallion along with a number of mares, foals, and young stock. When the young males grew old enough to become a threat to the stallion they were chased away and formed little bands, keeping to themselves until they could either persuade a few mares to come under their leadership or could take over the herd of a stallion that had grown too old to be able to defend his own band.

But the type of attack which occurs when a strange animal comes into the stable for the first time is not intended to hurt him, merely to make him keep his distance. After a few days he is accepted by the others and generally finds another animal that will pair off with him in the pasture—often the next most recent arrival.

Many horses that tend to kick and bite when ridden in pairs are doing so because they have never before been trained to be ridden close to another horse and are afraid. The cure is to choose two horses that are neither bad tempered nor timid, then, with good riders on all three, to ride the belligerent horse between the other two in very close order. After a few minutes at the sitting trot and later work at the strong trot and the canter it will be found that the erstwhile refactory horse soon loses his fears and is quite happy to work in company. The horse that kicks not from fear but from bad temper can be cured the same way. He will not dare to start a fight with a horse on each side giving him no way to escape from retaliation.

Should you find yourself in a situation where you want to ride in a pair with another rider and are on a bad-tempered animal which has never been trained out of his habit, you can still do so safely by using the following method.

To begin with, it should be understood that aggressive horses tend either to bite or to kick but seldom try both methods, except in some cases when charging a person on foot. If your horse is a biter, ride him slightly in advance of your partner and bend his head away from the latter. The indirect rein is best (left rein to the left to bend his head but tension in front of the withers toward your own right hip; this applies when you are riding to the left of your partner). Punish any sign of misbehavior with a sharp lift upward on one rein together with a slap of your crop on his right shoulder. If he tends to kick, ride slightly behind (the width of the horse's head) and bend his head slightly toward your partner. When he shows signs of kicking, hold his head up with both reins and use a spur or the crop just behind the saddle girth the instant he misbehaves. Afterward, quiet the animal and return him to his former position.

Young and inexperienced riders should be trained, when two aggressive horses start a kicking match, to immediately bring their heads together with the strong use of both reins and legs. They should never try to ride them away from each other, as this keeps their rumps in the perfect position to go on kicking.

Occasionally one finds a horse that is not actually mean, but that does not like horses coming up too close from behind, or may even take a dislike to all horses of a certain color or marking. Such animals rarely give trouble under good riders and for this reason it is very difficult to break them of the habit as, under experienced hands, butter wouldn't melt in their mouths. If a beginner has to be mounted on such a horse he should be put last in line. At some time the instructor or trainer might get on the disobedient horse and demonstrate that he or she (and it is often a mare) will behave well under experienced hands, explaining that the beginner will also learn to do this in time. These animals are not acting from fear, nor, as a rule, from meanness; they just want to establish themselves as rulers of the herd, or at least as being very high up in the pecking order.

Let me repeat that, regarding aggressiveness in horses and ponies, I have never known one that would kick or bite at both humans and equines. In fact, sometimes the horse that is bad tempered with his mates will go out of his way to be protective toward humans, especially children.

THE SULKY OR STUBBORN HORSE

We come now to the obstinate, stubborn, or sulky horse. This is usually an insensitive animal with a thick hide which has learned to resist by refusing to obey rather than by active aggression. The cause may be fear or it can be the result of bad or insufficient training. Another common cause is being ridden by inexperienced riders who do not have sufficient control over their own bodies to be able to control the horse. With jumping horses it can be the result of being asked to jump too high or being asked to practice for such long periods that the horse becomes terribly fatigued without the rider being aware of it. Boredom is still another cause of balkiness.

Yet this very lack of sensitivity makes the "cold-blooded" an-

At the strong and at the extended trot the horse drops his head and pushes with his quarters, his front legs reaching forward.

imal which has a preference for standing still rather than for running away in moments of stress valuable as a beginner's mount. Properly trained, he can become one.

The first thing to do is to make him move out at once on demand. If he is bitted correctly and if riders are taught what to do when he is disobedient he will eventually forget his bad habits, but until he does so he should be ridden only by capable riders.

This type of horse will need to be schooled until he moves out automatically at the slightest application of the legs or back. The best exercise is that of teaching him smooth and immediate transitions from one gait to another and from the slow phase of each gait to the ordinary or strong phase of the same gait. He must be taught to go "on the bit," to extend or collect as needed, and to turn readily both to the left and to the right in circles and half circles while bending his body evenly from poll to dock.

In demanding the transitions, practice until the horse, being at a collected, sitting trot, moves out immediately in an ordinary trot when the rider pushes with his back and follows with his reins. From that he is trained to drop his head and push with his quarters, reaching forward with his front legs until he is in at least a strong trot and preferably an extended trot. He must come back to the ordinary trot inside a stride or two and to the collected trot the same way. When he knows all his gaits and will extend and collect easily he can be taught to take only six or eight steps of each phase before changing to a different phase. Also, the order of the phases should not always remain the same: posting trot to collected, to strong to collected, for example, and the same in the canter and the walk. As for the transitions, the ideal is for the horse to take up any gait from any other gait or from the halt and to return to the original gait at once.

The test of the success of the training is the reduced resistance of the horse. Originally it may be found necessary to use spurs quite strongly or to give a cut with a crop on the barrel if the horse is really stubborn about moving out, but when he finds out that disobedience brings punishment and obedience reward in the form of lighter aids, he will soon yield to the rider.

Some stubborn horses acquire the habit of backing up when they don't want to go forward. The most effective cure is to rein them back immediately, making them step as fast as possible,

We now come to the obstinate, stubborn, or sulky horse.

for fifty or sixty feet in a straight line or until they give up and are willing to move forward. Usually one such session is enough but if not, simply repeat the treatment until the horse realizes that refusal to move out on demand will bring a punishment which is far from comfortable.

Don't forget, after demanding something, anything at all, from a horse—meeting resistance and applying whatever punishment is necessary—when the horse capitulates, immediately reward him with a tidbit, a kind word or a pat, and perhaps a few minutes at the walk on a long rein. In this way he will associate good behavior with a reward and bad behavior with punishment.

When the time comes to allow less experienced riders to ride an animal that previously had any of the above-mentioned bad habits but is now considered cured, be sure the rider you choose is capable of handling him, that he carries a crop or switch, and that you have instructed him in exactly what to do should his mount revert to his old ways.

III

Problems Arising From Confusion

When a human being is faced with problems which he feels forced to solve and which he cannot solve, especially in cases in which the solution which he believes to be the normal one turns out to have completely incomprehensible results, he may end up with a severe nervous breakdown. In part, this can be due to over-sensitivity or insecurity within himself, plus the frustration of not being able to accomplish what he has set out to do. Or it may result from his inability to come up with any workable solution to a problem which is of vital importance to him. He starts by being irritable, then, as the tension builds up, he becomes unreasonable and excitable to the point of hysteria. His fears become illogical and he overreacts to the slightest frustration.

Now let us consider the horse, a highly sensitive and nervous animal, and what happens to him under similar circumstances.

If he is a valuable animal, destined perhaps for the show ring or for sale to the rider who is highly skilled, the horse has been trained to respond immediately to a very light application of the aids. He has learned their "language" thoroughly under the hands of his trainer. Suddenly he finds himself ridden by an inexperienced rider who has never learned this language. Up until now this rider has ridden only thick-skinned mounts that have slow reactions and heavy mouths. Our sensitive horse is accustomed to move out at once on feeling the slightest possible pressure of the legs of his rider and a little push with his seat, and, as he starts forward, hands that follow without losing the light tension on the bit. Instead of receiving the signals to which he has been trained, he now receives a thumping and painful application of the legs of this new rider, and perhaps even the sharp dig with the spur. Naturally he bounds forward automatically, to be hauled in by a heavy hand and to feel the weight of his insecure rider shifting first this way and then that as the latter tries to maintain his balance. Nor does the agony of the pressure on his delicate bars cease when he halts abruptly. It continues, for the rider is now depending on his reins to keep from falling off. The totally confused animal may move backward or even rear.

If this ignorant and inexperienced rider is taken off the horse immediately the latter will soon get over his fright under the calm, light hands of the experienced rider. But if such treatment continues, this horse, like the human being subjected to too much stress and confusion, as well as being faced with impossible situations for which his training and earlier experience have not prepared him, will also suffer a type of nervous breakdown. He will become more and more excitable and, finally, hysterical.

I have quoted an extreme case. But a horse that is very sensitive may also be reduced to a bundle of nerves if ridden by a fairly expert rider who has never ridden highly sensitive animals and who uses his legs and hands too strongly without releasing immediately when the horse begins to respond. Eventually such horses become so nervous as to become dangerous or, at the least, unusable for ordinary riding.

However, the cure is comparatively simple, and always effective, although it may take a long time.

The first thing to do is to restore the horse's calmness and confidence in his rider, along with his immediate, ingrained obedience. To do this we return to the simple lessons and exercises to which he was introduced after he had learned oral language on the longe. But remember, he has meanwhile developed tensions and fears which he never had before, and so the progress will be much slower.

The most common fear will be fear of the bit. This will result

Fear of the bit results in a stiffening of the poll and a high carriage of the head as the horse attempts to evade the demands of the rider's hands.

in stiffness in the poll and jaw, an attempt to avoid the bit by throwing the head up and the nose in the air. The neck, instead of bending on a convex curve beginning just behind the poll, will dip. The horse will have developed an "upside-down" neck and the rider will feel that his mount is trying to "put his ears in his lap." He has become a "star-gazer." The opposite reaction is for the horse to try to get "behind the bit" by bringing his head in to his chest and "boring." This is a very difficult vice to cure and leads to developing a bend in the neck almost half-way to the withers. It may become necessary to rig up an overhead check rein which fastens to the two rings of the snaffle, is brought up under the brow band and headpiece, then down to a ring or strap fastened on the front of the pommel of the saddle. In adjusting it care should be taken to see that it becomes uncomfortable only when the horse drops his head below the normal head-carriage at the walk. This horse is not afraid of the bit; he is more apt to be an animal which is inclined to be heavy going and sluggish but which, through confusion due to bad training, has developed this vice to escape heavy hands.

For the nervous, high-strung animal with a real fear of the bit the best thing to do is take the bit out of his mouth and ride him in an English style hackamore. This type of hackamore consists of a wide, padded noseband, adjustable in size, a chain which may or may not be covered, and two aluminum cheekpieces which are about four inches long and slightly curved. The hackamore is attached to the headstall of an ordinary snaffle bridle in the usual fashion except that the nose band is fitted somewhat lower than the ordinary cavesson, being about three finger widths below the cheekbones; the chain will be somewhat higher. The rider will find that he has plenty of control, and with no bit in his mouth and the pressure only on his nose, the horse will soon drop his head and lose his fear.

Occasionally we find a horse that is so stiff behind the poll, either from fear or because he has never been trained properly, that he doesn't seem to understand what is wanted of him when the rider tries to bring his head in with the reins, and moves backward instead. A good method to cure this is to stand by the horse's head with a bit of apple in your left hand and with your right hand grasp the reins six inches behind his chin; then entice

The overhead check to prevent boring. This can also be used to prevent ponies from grazing when ridden by incompetent riders.

The English type hackamore. Useful for initial training of the young horse both on the lunge line and under the saddle. Also for reschooling the horse that is afraid of the bit.

Teach the horse to flex at the poll by using a tidbit.

him by brushing his lips with the apple and carrying your hand back as you supple his poll by gently vibrating the reins and pulling them backward. When he bends even a little, reward him with the apple and continue the practice with another piece. When he begins to connect the bending of the poll, the apple, and the feel of the pressure on the nose band, the same thing can be done with the rider mounted. It usually takes a very short time to teach the horse to flex without resistance when using this method.

When he starts his training in the hackamore, the first goal of the trainer is to get his horse to walk along quietly on as long a rein as possible. In the beginning, the pupil will probably break the gait every few steps, throw his head, and feel very unsteady and uncadenced. He should be soothed with the voice and a pat and brought back quietly to the walk. Not until he is perfectly calm at the walk on a long rein should the rider collect the reins a little and get the horse accustomed to the feel of pressure on his nose when a halt is demanded. Sometimes a horse will walk for a certain distance on the straight, then tend to jog or try to canter. The rider should anticipate this, and when the horse collects under him the rider should bend him in a wide circle not less than 30 feet in diameter. This will serve to distract him and will also start his work on bending his body correctly. Only a very mild pressure of the leg at the knee and just below it should be used on these turns if the horse shows any excitement. Later he will learn to accept both the legs and the spur. This will be proof that his confidence in his rider has been restored.

To ask a horse to go forward the rider should use his back, let his hands follow, and say "walk." In halting he keeps his legs firmly on the horse and squeezes the reins as though he were squeezing water from a sponge. The squeezes should be in cadence with the horse's stride, with each squeeze a little stronger than the last until the horse has stopped; along with each squeeze goes a slight push with the back to bring the horse up into the bit and halt him with all four legs under his body. The voice can also be used on the final stride in a sharp tone. When the horse has stopped, the rider should relax his aids (reins, legs, and seat) and pat the horse on the shoulder. He must be made to stand for a moment and then move out again. If he is too restless

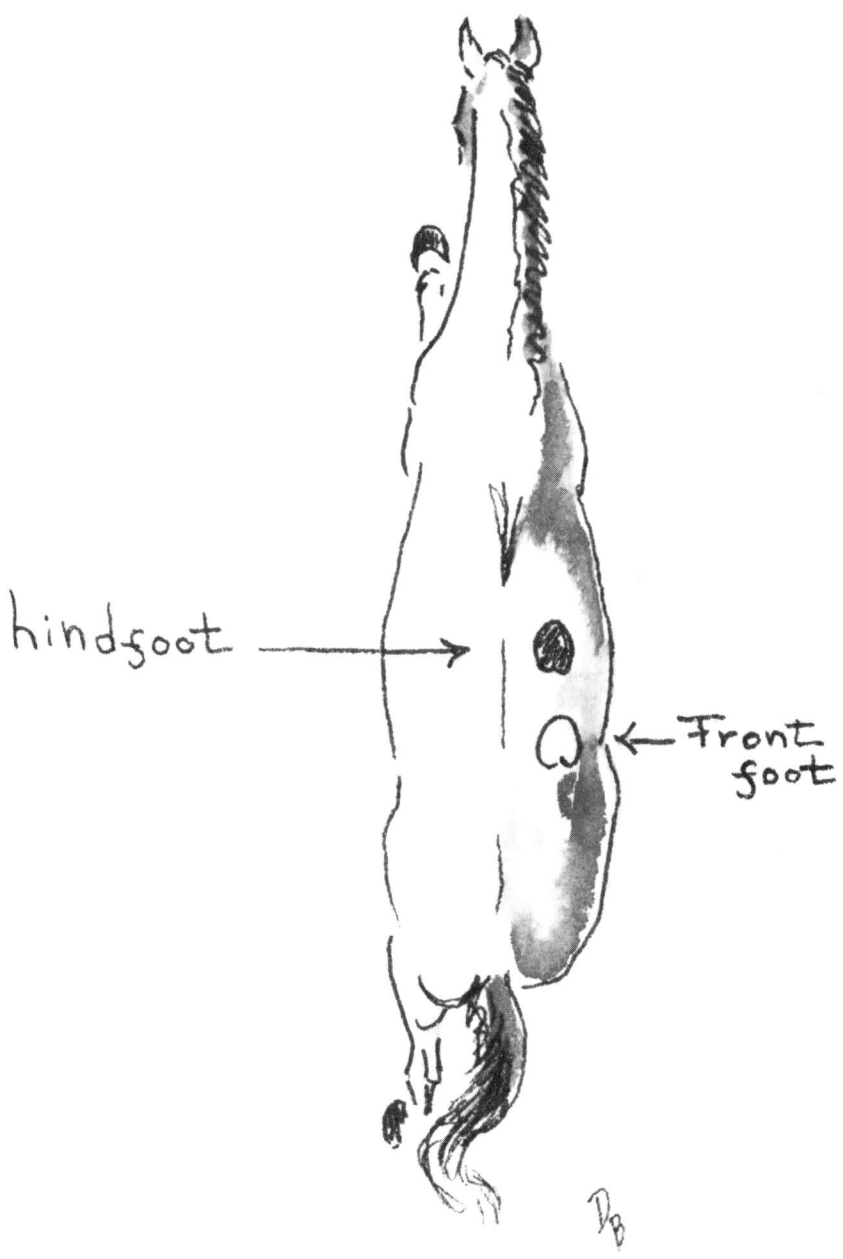

Diagram of the footprints of the horse at the extended trot. Notice that the back feet are placed in front of the front feet. Not all horses extend with as much overreach as shown here, but the print of the back foot must never be behind that of the front.

to stand still, a tidbit of carrot given from the saddle each time he stops will soon cure him.

When the horse will take long steps at the walk, dropping his head and swinging it naturally with no sign of nervousness or tendency to break into a trot, the sitting trot can be introduced. As the horse will now raise his head the reins should be shortened but no attempt should be made to bring his nose in any more than is natural to him. After trotting quietly for fifty feet or so he should be brought gently back to the walk, then halted and patted. If allowed to trot farther than this before he has learned that he need have no fear, he may, from nervousness, start to trot faster and faster. In this case it would not be possible to bring him down again without using aids which, being of necessity too strong, would disturb him and set his training back.

Circles, serpentines, and half turns, in which the rider performs a half circle fifteen feet in diameter, then rides back to the wall on a diagonal, should now be introduced. As the days go by and the horse responds without excitement, the rider can gradually take a firmer hold on the reins and use a little more back and stronger legs to induce the horse to bend properly in his turns and to bring his hindquarters under him.

However, before any more difficult work is attempted (such as the lateral movements, the collected canter, and so forth), the horse should be trained to move out on a strong trot. This will serve two purposes. It will loosen up the muscles of the loin and get the horse to use his whole body freely (a horse that is tense and nervous cannot do this—he can only take little, short, choppy steps) and it will allow him to go at a rapid rate of speed but one which will not excite him as would galloping.

The way to demand a strong trot or to train a horse which has never been trained to take one is to drop your hands below the level of the withers, separate your hands so that the reins do not touch any part of the body and take a firm hold, and then, with light, successive pressure of the legs, and perhaps a special word such as "hut!-hut!" given at each stride, urge the horse forward. Do not try to sit this trot. It is difficult to do so without disturbing the horse. Either post or keep a balanced position with your weight on your knees and stirrups only and your back hollowed and inclined forward. The buttocks are not pushed under but merely raised a few inches. The horse should lean slightly on the rider's hand of his own accord. This helps him to maintain his balance which is no longer over his center but pushed forward. It may take weeks or months to get a really strong trot from a horse that has never been trained in this before. Remember that the cadence or beat of the gait is the same as that of the ordinary and collected phases. The horse should not take short, quick steps but long strides.

There are two ways of measuring the increase in the length of the stride and thus determining the success of the exercise. One is to trot completely around the arena at the sitting trot, counting the number of steps the horse takes. Then do the same at the ordinary posting trot and finally at the strong or extended trot. Remember that at the sitting trot you are counting steps, not strides, so in posting you will have to count each time you go up and each time you sit. There should be definitely fewer steps as the gait becomes longer and stronger: perhaps a hundred steps at the sitting trot, seventy to eighty at the ordinary, and as few as fifty or sixty at the strong.

The second method of checking is to look at the horse's hoofprints. In order to lengthen his stride the horse must push his hindquarters under him and bend all three joints of his back legs (stifle, hock, and ankle). A horse that is stiff in either loin or joints will not be able to push his haunches under him to lengthen his stride. The prints of the trot at any phase of such a horse will show that the print of the hind foot is perceptibly behind the print of the front foot on the same side. As he learns to flex his joints correctly and to develop a supple back and loin the back print will be on top of the front. In the extended trot it will often be well ahead of it. A big difference will also be noticed in the smoothness of the trot, since the horse that does not flex his joints and relax his back trots as though his legs were stiff pegs—making it very hard for the rider to keep contact with the saddle at the sitting trot.

The sensitive rider can also feel when the horse is using himself correctly at the strong and extended phases as the haunches will swing fluently from side to side under him and the movement will be rhythmical and so light that there is scarcely any sound to the hoofbeat.

Letting the horse walk on a long (stretched) rein to teach him to maintain that gait without having to be held in.

The canter should not be introduced until the horse is thoroughly calm at all phases of the trot on a long rein and will come down without excitement to a halt. He will now probably benefit by practice in the more advanced equitation exercises. These include pivots around the haunches and pivots around the forehand. One step at a time should be demanded and the horse halted between each. This induces him to wait for the command of the rider and not to whirl around on his own; it also enables the rider to control the haunches and forehand individually. Later the horse will step around without halting, but with a cadenced step, he pivot leg being lifted and replaced as the other legs perform the circle.

He is also ready to work on smooth transitions from one phase of a gait to another and from one gait to the another: walk to sitting trot, walk to posting trot, sitting trot to strong trot and back to the orginal gait, as well as halt to trot and back with no intervening walking steps.

If the horse has had previous dressage training or if the rider is familiar with these exercises, one of the very best ways to get the horse to accept the bit, to pay attention, and to be obedient and flexible is through the lateral movements. These include the shoulder-in, leg-yielding, the two-track or half-pass, and the counter-change of hands on the two-track. These are all done at the sitting trot with as much collection as the horse is able to give. They are alternated every few minutes with asking the horse to move out on the strong trot or to walk on a loose rein.

All horses are born one sided. There is a stiff side toward which the horse finds it difficult to bend his body or to move laterally, and there is a hollow side. Some horses will not accept the bit properly on their hollow side but tend to flex their necks too much.

The young horse learns to perform turns, circles, and these lateral movements in both directions from the beginning of his training, thus becoming equally flexible on both sides. The older horse which has never been so trained and who has become confused or nervous finds this very hard. It may be next to impossible to get him to relax his stiff side completely, and one can only continue to work on it, going as far as possible and refusing to get discouraged.

The canter can be introduced as soon as the horse accepts the aids, has a good head carriage, and shows no resistance or excitement. At this time other and more difficult movements can also be introduced. These require that the horse bend his body from dock to poll, as in circling and in the shoulder-in, but whereas in the latter movement he was asked to move in the direction of the outer side of the curve, now he will be asked to move toward the inside of the curve. These movements are the "haunches-in" or *travers* and the "haunches-out" or *renvers*. Consulting any good book on advanced equitation will provide the reader with diagrams of the patterns of all these movements and describe the aids to be used in demanding them. The horse should be taught them on his hollow side first, and when he understands he can also be taught on his stiff side. Usually it will be necessary to work twice as hard and long on the stiff side as on the hollow. A good way is to begin with the stiff side, practice each movement once around the arena, then go to the hollow side, and finally repeat again on the stiff. When the horse has become very flexible and obedient with practice the various movements can be combined, shoulder-in to haunches-in, changing every six steps, for example, and keeping the horse curved in the same curve for both. Haunches-in to haunches-out is more difficult as the curve must now be reversed.

We started this work in a hackamore. How soon this can be dispensed with and the snaffle bit introduced will depend on the reactions of the horse. It is perfectly possible to teach all the dressage figures in a hackamore. The horse will develop excellent flexion of the poll, but he will not develop flexion of the gullet and lower jaw. A good way to make the transition is to put the snaffle on under the hackamore with side-reins attached to it. Adjustable side-reins are available, the front eighteen inches or so being made of elastic. They fasten to the bit and are carried back to the front billet strap of the girth. By fastening them in this manner, instead of around the girth, they will not slide down and put too much downward pressure on the horse's mouth. They should be adjusted loosely at first so that the horse feels no tension unless he throws his head up. When he has become accustomed to the feel, they can be tightened so that there is light pressure when he is walking and his head is extended. A few

The shoulder-in, as seen as the horse approaches the observer. Note that the inside back foot is being placed in line with the outside front foot.

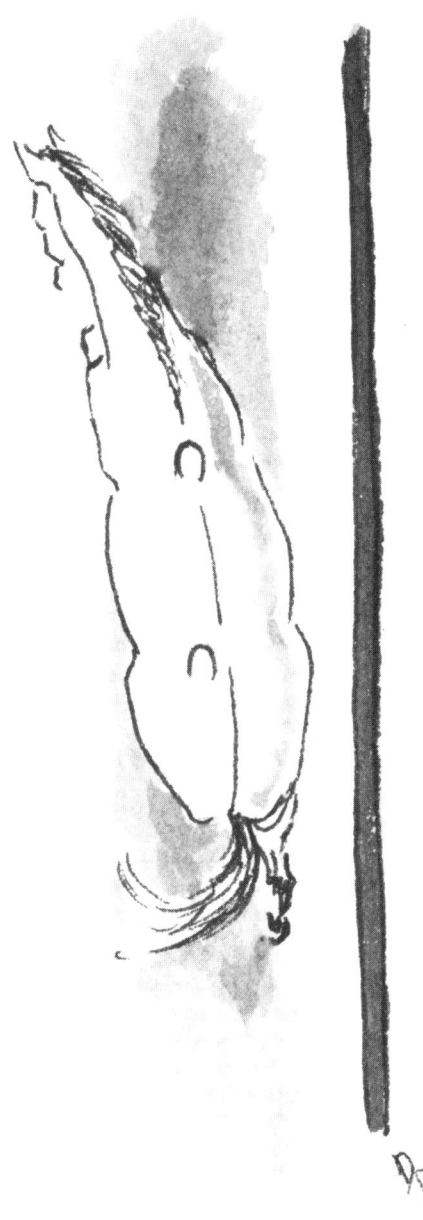

The diagram shows the even bending of the spine from poll to dock. The haunches are squarely on the track. The forehand is carried about 12 inches off the track toward the center. The bend of the neck is no stronger than that of the spine behind the withers. The most common error is for the uneducated rider to bend the horse's head and neck too strongly leaving the forehand on the track so that the prints of the back feet are on those of the front at the sitting trot.

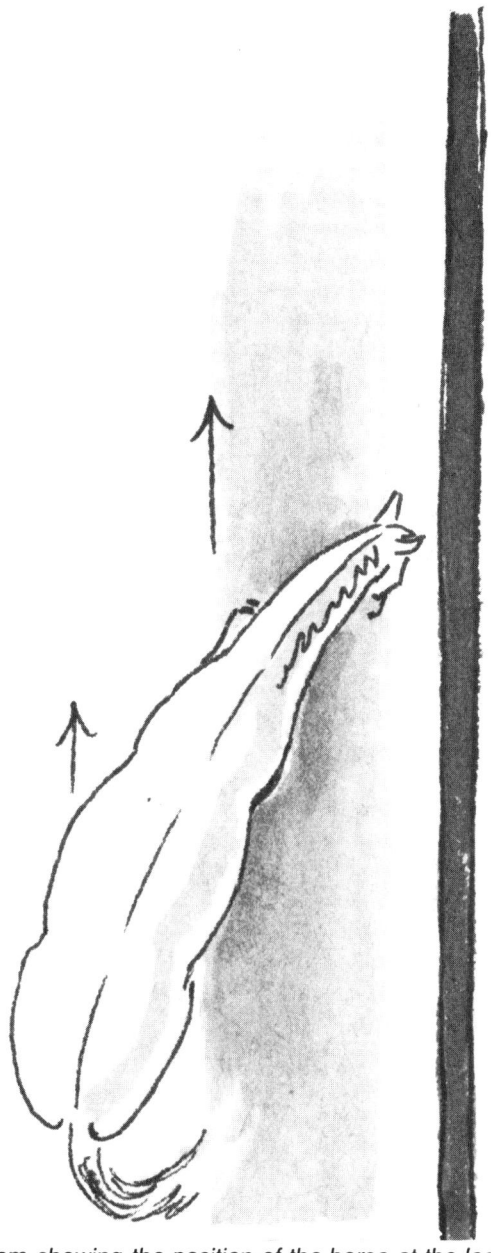

Diagram showing the position of the horse at the leg-yield. This movement is principally useful in teaching the horse to give way to the pressure of the rider's leg while in motion. It also serves to teach the intermediate rider to get the horse on the bit and keep him there.

The leg-yield as shown with the rider going away from the observer. Here the haunches are pushed to the center but there is no curve in the spine. The whole body is angled out from the wall and both the front and back legs cross.

The two-track or half-pass. The horse moves forward and sideways at the same time crossing both front and back feet. It can be practiced first as part of the half-turn. (See page 66.) Later the horse can be asked to execute the two-track after crossing the short wall of the arena and moving about ten feet on the track along the long wall at which point he leaves it on the two-track on a diagonal heading for the opposite corner. At first he is asked only to go as far as the center line. There he is straightened, ridden forward a few steps and then moved back to the original long wall on the two-track reaching it ten feet from the corner and continuing on the track. Later he may be asked to go all the way from one corner to that diagonally opposite.

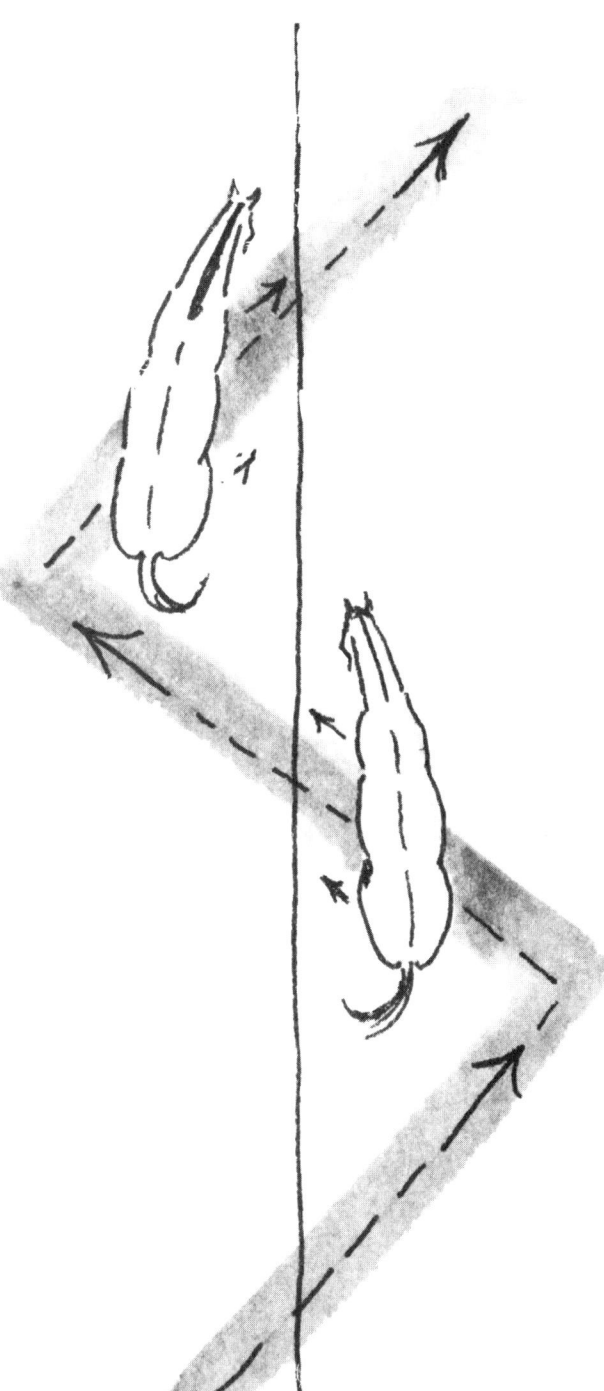

The counter-change of hands on the two-track. This is a zigzag pattern with the horse moving back and forth across the center line on the two-track and changing direction about every eight steps. Notice that the spine does not bend and that the head is always held slightly in the direction of the movement. The horse's body should be parallel to the long wall though his forehand may lead the haunches by a few inches.

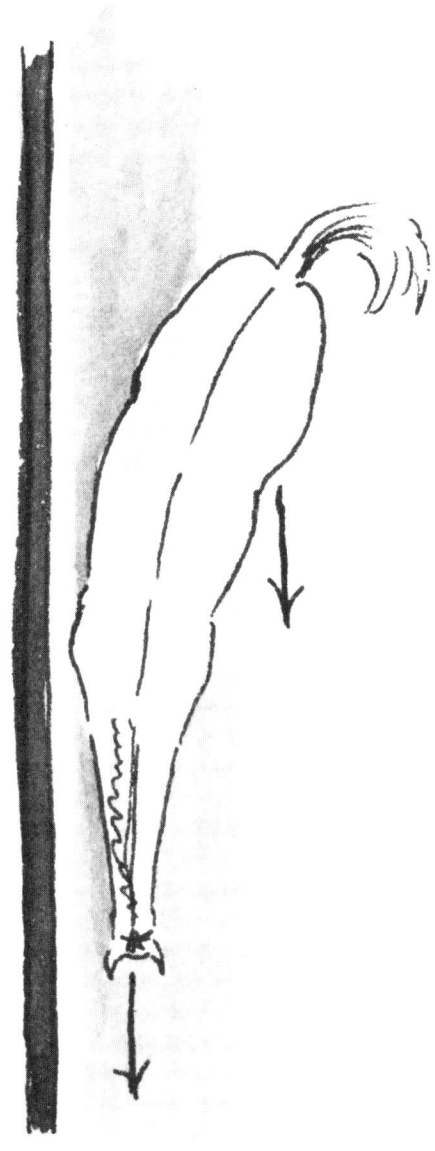

The travers. The horse's haunches are carried off the track toward the center. His spine is evenly curved and he moves toward the inside of this curve instead of toward the outside as in the shoulder-in. A very difficult movement.

Position of the horse at the travers in relation to the wall. Note that the forehand is now squarely on the track.

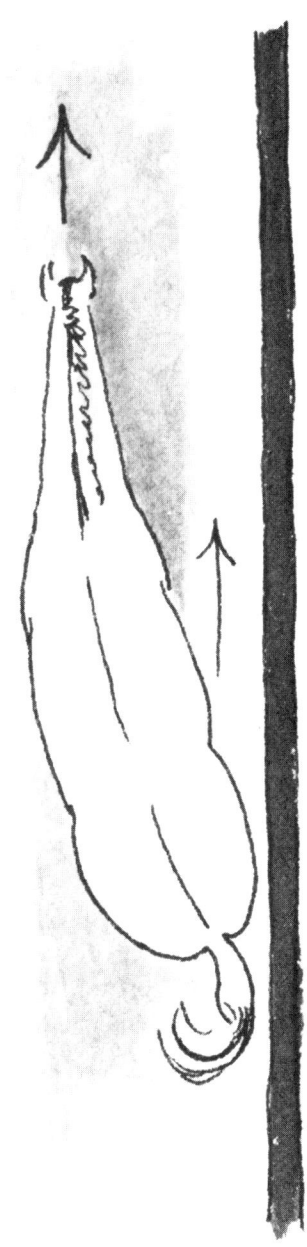

Position of the horse on the renvers in relation to the wall.

The renvers. Here the horse again moves toward the inside of the curve of his body but the forehand is carried in from the wall and parallel to it while the haunches are pushed out.

days of this and the rider can dispense with the side-reins and put ordinary reins on the bit. He now rides with four reins, using the snaffle more and more as the horse becomes accustomed to it and learns to relax his jaw when the reins are squeezed. When he will lean on the snaffle at the strong trot and come down to a halt without boring, opening its mouth, or tossing his head, the hackamore can be discarded.

The test of the successful training of the animal who was once a problem horse is his willingness to work quietly with any rider who has good hands and quiet legs.

CONFUSION DUE TO BAD TRAINING METHODS

The most common mistake which riders with insufficient experience in the methodical training of the young horse make is to rush his schooling. This is particularly true of jumpers. However this can also be true of ambitious riders who are anxious to teach their horses collection and advanced dressage figures before the horses have learned to extend their gaits, to accept the bit, respond to the legs, execute simple circles and turns to the right and left without resistance and with the proper curve, and to have smooth transitions from one gait to the other and from one phase of a gait to a different phase.

The sequence of training figures suggested in the aforementioned system of handling the hysterical horse should be followed when training the young horse. If this is not done, and the training of the horse is rushed, he will become confused. This will lead to a tendency to try to escape the bit and reins due to the horse's not understanding or not being capable of doing what is demanded of him. The resistance may take the form of boring, bracing, refusing to move forward or laterally at all, rearing, or plunging. All of this can be avoided if the training periods are never so long as to overtire the still undeveloped muscles of the young horse, never working at the same exercise so long that the horse becomes bored, and never going on to a more difficult movement until the simpler ones are performed smoothly and willingly in both directions. Sometimes it may be necessary to break up the lessons and not try to teach any movement that seems difficult without devising ways to make it easier. The

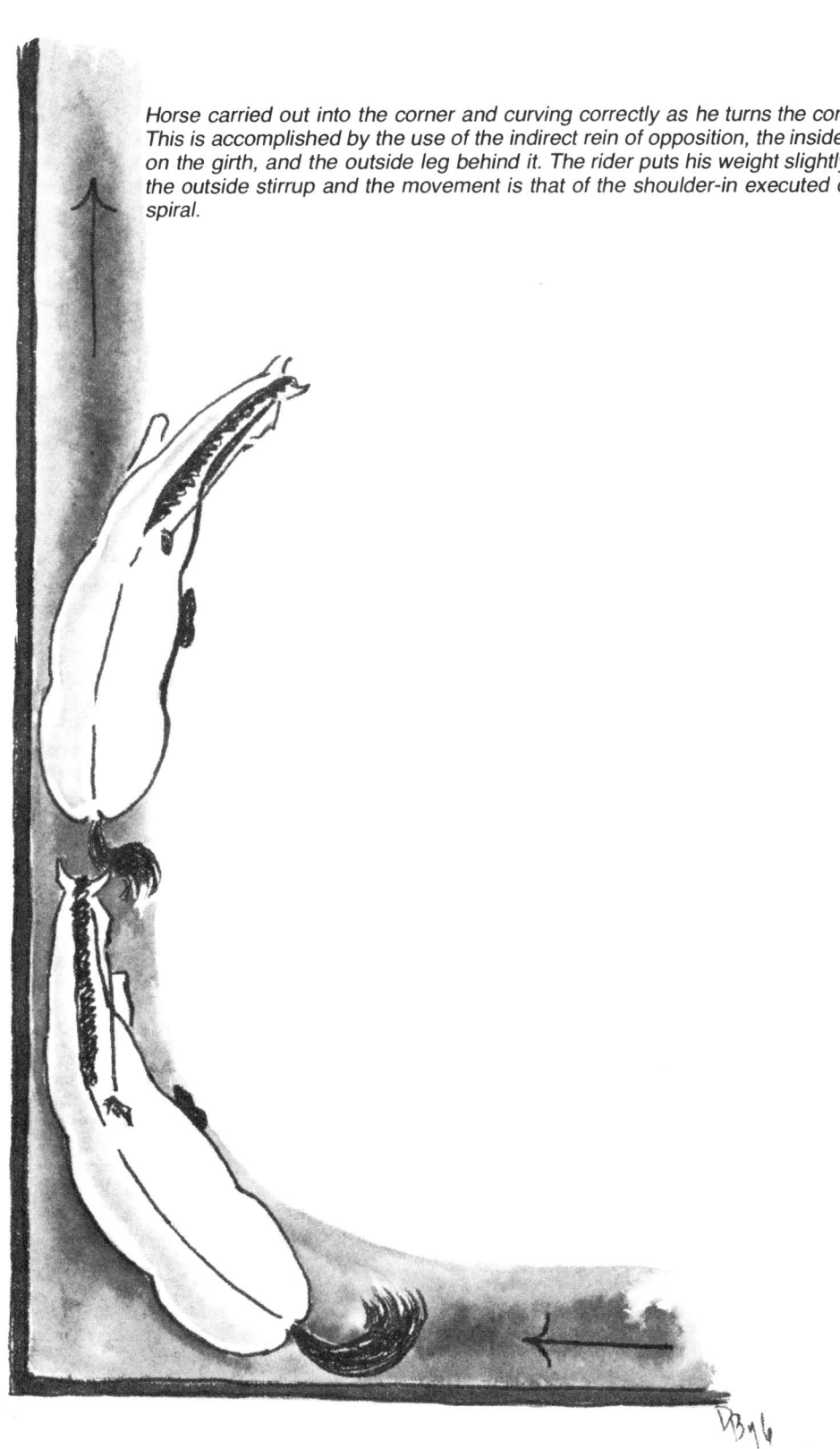

Horse carried out into the corner and curving correctly as he turns the corner. This is accomplished by the use of the indirect rein of opposition, the inside leg on the girth, and the outside leg behind it. The rider puts his weight slightly on the outside stirrup and the movement is that of the shoulder-in executed on a spiral.

Adjustment of the side-reins. These are used to teach the horse that when he carries his head correctly there will be no strong pressure on the bars of his mouth. But if he tosses his head or carries it too high it will be uncomfortable. However he will also learn that by yielding he automatically receives his reward by instant slackening of the pressure.

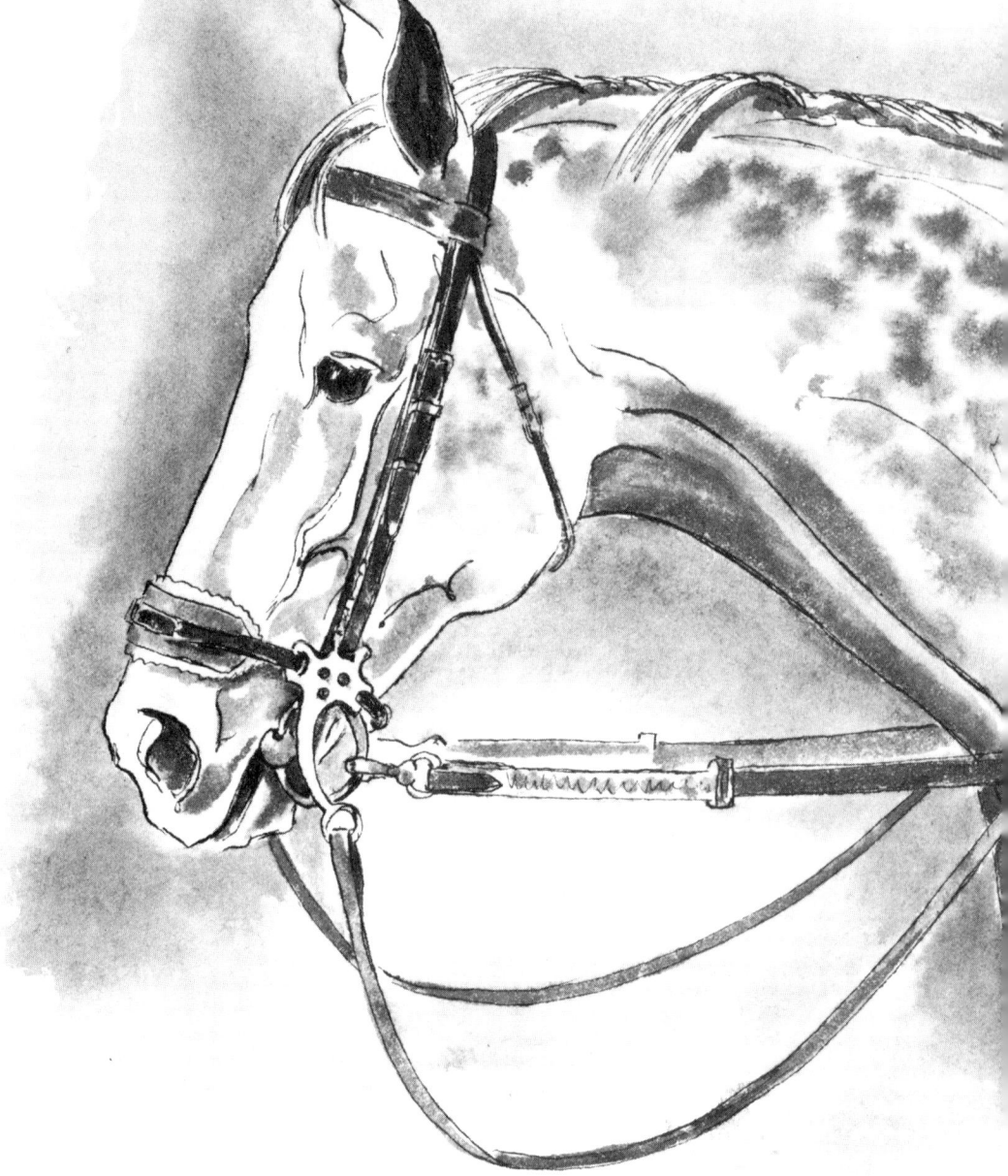

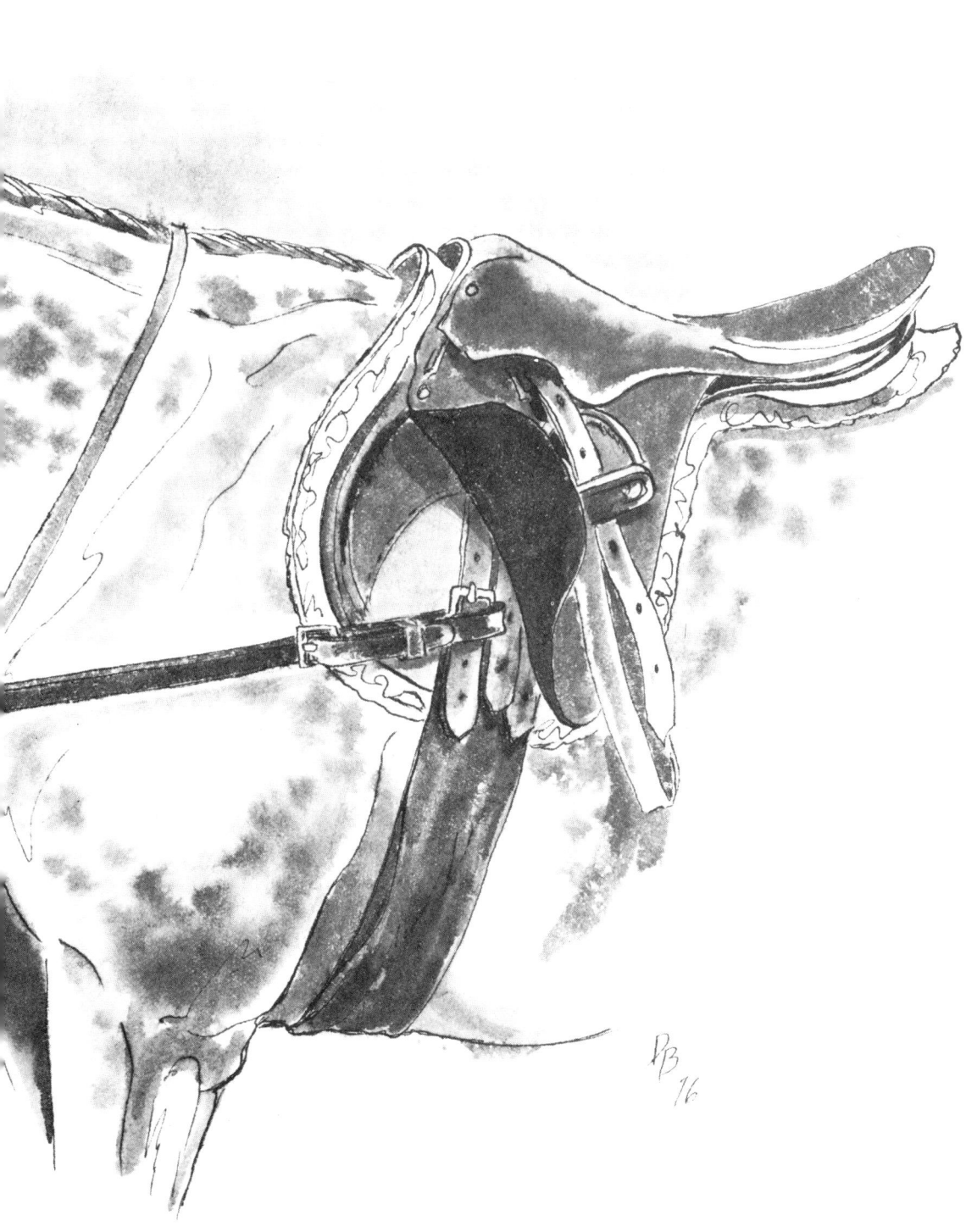

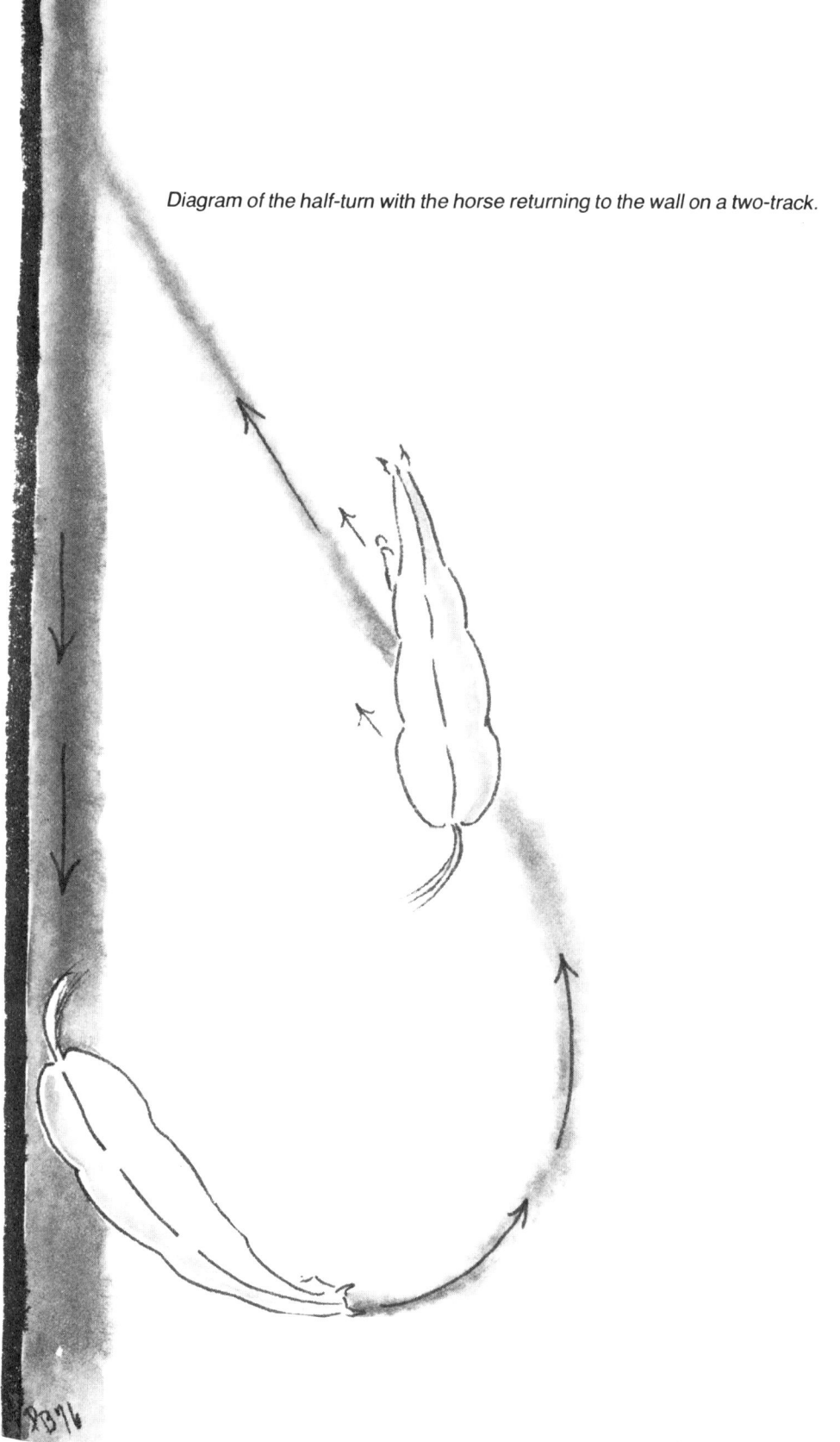
Diagram of the half-turn with the horse returning to the wall on a two-track.

shoulder-in can be demanded as the horse turns a corner by continuing the turn, keeping the bend of the body until the inside foreleg is off the track, and then starting the lateral movement but holding it for only four or five steps. Similarly, the two track can be taught by starting with a half turn and then two-tracking the few steps that will take the horse back to the wall on the diagonal rather than asking him to go from one wall to the center line. Sometimes a young horse will learn much more quickly if a rider on another horse works on the same movements while riding ahead of him on the track. This gives the pupil confidence and the impulse to continue moving in the desired direction. Like children, horses have definite personal aptitudes and difficulties, and the experienced and wise trainer will consider each as an individual and adjust his program accordingly.

TRAINING THE YOUNG OR THE PROBLEM JUMPER

The careful and methodical training of the horse destined to become a show jumper or a hunter is particularly important. The goal is to produce a horse that will jump smoothly, willingly, and quietly, will never refuse or attempt to shy out even though the jump may be one to which he is not accustomed, and will be under such control that he can be turned in any direction immediately on landing or stop smoothly if asked to do so at any time—whether approaching or leaving an obstacle. Horses that race wildly at their jumps, shy out unexpectedly, cannot be turned without using strength, and refuse to be rated are all the results of bad or too rapid training. Under a strong rider they may get over the jumps, but on difficult courses the wider circles which they will have to take in order to make the required turns will cost them more in time lost than those of the horse that moves more slowly but can be turned easily.

The horse that jumps from fear of the rider's spurs is not a safe horse. He cannot use his haunches correctly, he cannot judge the take-off as he should since his mind is on those spurs, and although he may succeed in clearing the obstacles the day will come when he will have a bad crash. Furthermore, if he is taught to use his haunches and listen to his rider he will be able to jump much higher than will ever be possible when he is

A bad approach to an obstacle. The horse has come in too fast and is fighting the bit with a stiff neck and poll. The departure will be rough and jerky and though he may get over the bars he will not be able to use his head properly and will probably land stiffly.

allowed to tear into his jump at a racing gallop.

The general rule either in beginning the training of a young jumper or in reschooling a ruined one is to start by scattering a number of low jumps, 12 to 18 inches in height, all around an arena. They should be so placed that there is plenty of room to circle between and around them and to come at them from either direction. The horse is then ridden calmly in and out and around these low obstacles at the walk and the sitting trot. He is brought up to them, stopped and allowed to sniff them then turned and moved on without jumping. When he no longer shows any excitement he can be popped quietly over them one at a time, and then turned away and circled around a different obstacle before being allowed to take a third located in a different part of the arena. Every now and then he should be brought up to the bar and stopped without being allowed to jump. All obstacles should be taken several times from both directions. If the horse has never jumped before at all, one end of each obstacle should be dropped to the ground. Before any of this work begins he should have been trotted over cavaletti on the ground and perhaps lunged over low jumps without a rider so that he knows what an obstacle is.

When he shows that he is calm the program can be varied slightly. Some jumps can be turned into spread jumps. If the course was originally one foot in height, the bars on some obstacles can be raised to eighteen inches. Flat boards can be leaned against the bars to imitate low chicken coops, while some obstacles can be formed of two crossed bars with the ends two feet high and the resulting cross about fourteen inches high at the center. Take-off bars set in front of other obstacles will encourage the young horse to stand back.

During this time the horse should be jumping from the trot. If he breaks into a canter after jumping, as he very probably will, he should not be pulled up sharply but should be quietly brought back to a trot before being allowed to take another obstacle.

When the horse is completely calm and will go up to the jump and either turn away when asked to, stop when asked to, or jump when the rider signals with his legs, carrying his body forward as the horse springs and following with his hands when he turns after jumping, and stops or continues as commanded, he

This rider is riding a course which demands a turn to the right. To achieve this he has placed his weight on his right stirrup at the height of the parabola of the jump and is looking toward the next obstacle. Thus prepared the horse will land on the right lead and be ready to make the required change in direction.

can be allowed to jump from the canter. This is first introduced by setting two obstacles in line with each other, two canter strides apart. The horse trots up to the first, is given a slight push as he lands so that he continues in a canter, canters over the second, and is then brought back to a trot.

Practice of this sort continues until the horse is willing to take three obstacles in a row without racing. However, until the rider tells him he must never know whether he is to continue over the three or whether the rider will pull out between them. The rider indicates his desires by giving light squeezes with his legs on each stride as he approaches a jump which he intends to take and gives the verbal command "off" with a harder squeeze when he wants the horse to jump. When he doesn't want the horse to take a jump ahead of him he sits down in the saddle and with the outside leg and the inside rein directs the horse away from the obstacle toward which he is heading, still in the canter which the horse has taken up after the preceding obstacle.

The time has now come for the rider to prepare the horse to change direction after a jump. This is done by stepping on one stirrup or the other as the horse is in the air over the obstacle. This will bring the horse down on the desired lead and enable him to turn smoothly. As always, the rider should be looking at the jump toward which he is heading as he takes the previous one.

By this time the horse should be willing to maintain a canter or a trot without racing or bracing, he should turn smoothly, take obstacles up to two feet in height in any order commanded by the rider, and remain under absolute control of the rider at every step.

When reschooling horses that have gotten into the bad habit of rushing or pulling, another very good exercise to be used when the horse is ready for slightly higher jumps is to put one jump up along the wall of the arena, then have the horse perform a series of circles inside this jump. The diameter of the circle should form a continuous line with the bars of the obstacle. If the horse is to be following a track to the left, he should circle to the left. When the horse is perfectly calm and the rider feels that the horse is ready to take the obstacle, he simply widens and slightly enlarges the circle as he approaches the takeoff side of the jump.

Brought in in this way the horse will take it calmly and he should then be cantered quietly along the track away from the jump, turned on the opposite side of the ring by means of a half turn, returned to the jump and circled again, this time to the right, and the exercise repeated.

When the horse jumps calmly and willingly, the jump can be raised, three or four inches at a time, but the instant he tends to get excited or jumps unwillingly the height should be dropped or the horse should return to the circling exercises.

Horses jump more willingly when following one another and have more confidence in their ability to clear the obstacle. However, they should not have this practice until the riders can rate them so that they can keep two- or three-length distances between each horse. They also learn to jump calmly when asked to take low jumps with two lines of horses coming in opposite directions, varying this with having them jump in pairs, threes, or fours, and in having them jump as teams of hunters. In this exercise, they start one behind the other (three horses make a team), take part of a course, all halt at the sound of a whistle and change places so that a different horse leads, and finish by coming up and taking the last jump abreast.

Having gotten your horse to jump quietly, don't make the mistake of over-jumping him so that he becomes tired. There is a terrific strain on the front legs of the horse each time he lands after even a low jump when he has a rider on his back. If his legs begin to hurt or feel tired he will respond by becoming either balky or excited.

Besides becoming sour from fatigue, horses also begin to be inattentive, careless, and disobedient from boredom. Their training should therefore be varied. Work over cavaletti placed on the ground will add variety to the program in the early stages of the horse's training. Cross-country riding over low field jumps in hunt formation does much to keep the horse fresh and interested, but the main thing is not to over-jump him by asking him to take too many high jumps in one session which are a strain on his legs and tendons.

Another cause of previously well-behaved horses becoming resistant is being used by beginners who cannot yet keep their balance and rhythm over the hurdles without pulling on the mouths of their mounts or coming back on the horses' loins with a thump. In our school we avoid this by using hackamores on all horses used for this work and never using horses that are extremely sensitive until the rider's skills have improved. Furthermore, we start by having the riders jump without saddles (which is easier than with a saddle over low jumps) and the horses wear neck straps which the riders slip their fingers under as the horse takes off. Later they take low jumps with their hands extended sideways at shoulder height. Only when their seats have become completely independent of reins and stirrups are the riders allowed saddles and bits in their bridles.

Let us summarize by saying that the well-trained horse listens to his rider at all times and that the experienced rider helps and never hinders his mount.

THE HORSE THAT HAS BEEN BRED AND TRAINED FOR RACING

Quite often a horse that has been trained for racing, but found to be not quite fast enough, is offered for sale at a very low price. Horses that have raced but have suffered bowed tendons are also frequently put up on the auction block, bought by dealers, and later sold as potential or even well-mannered hacks. Only a person experienced both in schooling young horses and in reschooling difficult animals should be tempted to buy such a horse. Aside from the possibility of previous injuries making the future of the retired race horse problematical, there is a difference in the basic training that he has received and in the habits that he has formed.

Take the Thoroughbred. This horse is extremely sensitive by nature. He has been ridden enough to get the worst of his youthful bucking and playing out of him. He has been trained to start fast at the gallop, to stop, to increase and decrease his stride, and not to object to mud flying in his face or to having to weave in and out and around a mass of flying bodies. He knows nothing of handling himself at the collected or ordinary gaits. He does not have lateral flexibility, nor does he respond to the more delicate uses of the aids. He knows how to run.

Next we have the brush-racer and the steeple-chaser. These

The young rider's first jump. The pony is bitted in a hackamore. The rider rides without a saddle so that the pressure on the stirrups will not cause her to be thrown too high and she has the further security of a neck strap which she can hold.

horses are not so apt to suffer from bowed tendons as they do not start their early training while their bones are still soft. But they, too, know only one thing: to go as fast as possible over a row of hurdles or around a course of varied field obstacles.

Then we have the Standardbred horse. He has been bred and trained only to trot. There are pacers, to be sure, but that gait is completely unsuitable for riding. Few Standardbreds that have actually been raced in sulkies are bought as potential riding horses, but even an unbroken colt of this breed inherits his instinct to trot fast rather than to canter and teaching such an animal a collected canter can be a long and frustrating job.

As with the other problem horses which we have been discussing, the flat racer, the brush-racer, the steeple-chaser, and the Standardbred must all go back to basic training as previously described. They must be taught the simple circles, the phases of the gaits, the rating, the transitions, etc., before being introduced to the lateral movements. They must be trained so that they work equally well on the side on which they are stiff as on the hollow side. They must forget the purpose of their original training or breeding: to get someplace fast.

Sometimes finding the right bit may be a problem. Flat racers and steeple-chasers are usually ridden in snaffles. Yet, to them, the snaffle is a bit they can lean on. Pelhams and full bridles are too strong. Their reaction is to either try to get above or behind the bit, to throw their heads, and dance nervously. In such cases I have found the English hackamore described earlier to be a very satisfactory solution. Even the most spirited animal seems to respond to this better than to anything else.

Sometimes it seems as though the earlier habits cannot be broken; that the horse off the track will never settle down and listen to the trainer. I remember Oriole, an eight-year-old mare that had competed in hurdle races over brush. Her one idea was to take off, but in the hackamore she was controllable. I worked her for two months in the riding hall at the sitting trot and the walk. Even the feel of the posting trot encouraged her to want to go faster. The movements which seemed to calm her the most were the two-track, the counter change at the two-track, the leg yield, and the shoulder-in. She became well balanced and worked equally well in both directions. During the third month we worked on the ordinary and strong trots, and rating and transitions were added to our daily program.

At the end of three months I thought it safe to allow her the reward of a canter. I had in mind a quiet, collected gait, but Oriole had different ideas. Joyfully, she took off, and we circumnavigated the hall three times before I prevailed on her to stop by heading her directly towards a wall.

We went back to work at the sitting trot. However, two months from the date of that first wild burst of speed I had succeeded in schooling her to a slow canter so successfully that I rode her in a musical ride carrying a lance in one hand. At one point the other leader and I took positions in the center of the arena, planted the ends of our lances on the ground and, without letting go of them, cantered in circles around them while the other riders, moving in the opposite direction, cantered in two large circles around us.

I never attempted to jump this horse on outside courses or to hunt her, but she became one of our best stadium jumpers and delighted in our exhibitions of "mental hazard" jumping.

In courses of this type the obstacles are not necessarily very high, but are either very easy to avoid or of rather startling appearance. In the former class there might be a simple carpenter's sawhorse set well away from anything else and with no guide bars or wings to keep the horse from shying out. Two ordinary side chairs placed facing each other, or a wheelbarrow, or a bicycle turned upside down with the wheels spinning are other such obstacles. It takes a well-schooled horse to go right over the center of such obstacles when the temptation to shy out is so great.

Then there are things such as a hose spraying water, the rider being required to jump the arc of water instead of the hose. There is also a bar on which a row of pails is hung. In the pails there are loose rocks and the bar, instead of being placed on the customary standards, is carried by a couple of volunteers who trot toward the approaching horse rattling the pails. A clothesline hung with clothes blowing in the wind is another favorite. The *pièce de résistance* is the big iron hoop wrapped with burlap which had been soaked in kerosene and then set on fire. Oriole, my erstwhile brush-jumper, loved this one especially. I had only to head her for it and she would canter quietly toward it and straight through it, completely calm in the face of the flames. The long hours of slow schooling had paid off in the end.

Ariel, another favorite, was a two-year-old Standardbred who was completely unschooled when I got her. But she had generations of trotters behind her and it was not until she was pushing four that I finally taught her a collected canter. She also learned to jump, hunt, and drive, and won a number of "road-hack" classes in local shows.

In every case, patience and a willingness to proceed slowly are the factors which will bring success. Calmness and a willingness to listen to the rider are the first goals. When these are accomplished and the training is given methodically the rewards can be very great indeed.

IV

Everyday Problems to Be Expected When Working With Young or Partially Trained Horses

SHYING

It is the nature of all horses to be afraid of things that are unusual, especially objects that move, make rustling sounds, or those that they come upon suddenly. A man carrying an umbrella becomes a totally different creature to the young horse. Even one carrying a rake over his shoulder instead of in the usual position is transformed into a monster who is about to attack. A boy pushing a bicycle instead of riding it may frighten the colt that is accustomed to seeing children riding bicycles pass on the public road near his pasture. Every horse certainly knows what a wheelbarrow is, but the animal who is thoroughly accustomed to the sound and sight of this ordinary stable machine as it is rolled along an aisle will behave like an utter fool if he sees it standing in the center of the riding hall. Stupidity? In a sense, yes. But remember, had Eohippus stood his ground and waited to investigate the cause of the rustle in the grass or the appearance of an object with which he was not familiar, the race would never have survived.

One must also remember that the eyes of the horse work completely differently from ours. With his head raised he can see distant obstacles clearly, but not what is close to him. Nor are the separate images which he sees with each eye converted into one image by his brain: he sees them as separate images. And, because his eyes are widely separated, if he catches sight of a piece of paper on the side of the road first with one eye and then with the other it will appear to jump.

The earliest treatises on the horse and his training which still survive were written by Xenophon the Greek about 400 B.C. He understood the fears common in all young horses and advised that the grooms lead the colts and fillies daily through the marketplace so that they might become accustomed to strange sights and sounds before they were given more difficult training under the saddle.

Another fear which the horse has inherited from his primeval ancestors is the fear of stepping on anything strange. Many horses not trained out of this as foals or weanlings will refuse to walk through mudpuddles, or cross streams or bridges.

If, as a foal, the horse becomes accustomed to sights and sounds which are not normally part of the landscape, and if he is carefully trained to go where he is led, he will soon lose his fears.

If the pasture where the young stock are kept is near a public highway the foal will become accustomed to traffic the easy way. If the pasture is a distant one, mares with their foals should be brought into a paddock where the little fellows can see automobiles and trucks coming into the stable yard. With a calm mother standing by they will soon accept these odd looking creatures as commonplace and not to be feared.

Starting with when he is first halter-broken, which should occur before he is three weeks old, the young foal should be led through muddy places, streams, puddles, along wooden or cement aisles, through narrow doorways, up and down low steps and, if there is a horse van or trailer on the place, in and out of that. He will go readily if his mother precedes him. When he has lost all fear of unusual footing it will be found that he will not be afraid when asked to negotiate such obstacles even when not accompanied by the mare.

However, suppose one is faced with the three-year-old, newly broken to the saddle, perfectly obedient and mannerly in the schooling ring and adjacent trails and fields but with little experience on the road. One must remember the early training methods and ride him only in company until he has gained a little confidence. At first he will be behind or beside another horse. After a few such lessons, he should be asked to lead when returning home. His training in the ring should have taught him to move out at once when asked to and, if he understands the shoulder-in, this movement can be put to use if he meets something of which he is afraid when he is alone with no other horse to follow.

Needless to say, his first trips alone away from the stable should be along familiar roads or trails and he should not be kept out for over a half an hour. Be prepared for much nickering as he returns home.

Even with all this preparatory training the time will no doubt come when the rider on his young horse will meet something that is strange and frightening. The animal's head will go up, his ears will come forward, and his steps will shorten as he collects himself preparatory to whirling.

The first thing to remember is that punishment will only add the fear of pain to that of the unknown object and thus will make him doubly afraid and even more tense and hard to control. The rider should soothe him with his voice and urge him along with his legs, keeping his head straight, and making every effort to prevent him from stopping. If the object which he is afraid of is a stationary one, and if the colt knows the shoulder-in movement, he can often be induced to pass it in this position. If he should spin around suddenly, keep him turning and urge him forward as he completes the circle instead of trying to pull him back. Occasionally, the horse that has been well trained to rein back can be reined back until he is past the thing of which he is afraid.

If the object is approaching and the horse seems unduly terrified, signal to it to stop and then try to work the horse past it using the shoulder-in. If this doesn't work, take him off the road (or onto the shoulder if it is not possible to get entirely off), then beckon to the driver of the vehicle to pass slowly. Your colt will probably dance up and down, try to whirl, etc. Keep on calming him and keep him moving either in circles or sideways. Even if it

Training the foal to be unafraid of mounting a ramp.

takes all night you must not give up since the horse will eventually submit to your will. Perhaps you will be fortunate and a car will come along going your way. If the young horse sees a vehicle willing to pass whatever it is that scares him, nine times out of ten he will regain his confidence and will follow along behind. Having passed it and found that nothing very terrible happened he will be less frightened the next time. Under no circumstances should you dismount and try to lead him past the obstacle of which he is afraid, since he will only jerk away from you and it may be a long walk home.

We have spoken of what to do when a horse tries to resist by spinning or whirling. The same method is used with the horse which, not through fear but through stubbornness, refuses to go in the direction desired. His resistance takes the form of popping out his shoulder, bracing his neck, and bending his head in the direction you want him to go but moving away from it. Your solution is to reverse your aids, turn him the way he wants to go but spin him all the way around in a circle, then push him on before he has a chance to brace himself again.

One often meets up with this problem in dealing with the school horse who wants to turn down a familiar trail which will take him back to the stable, or the badly trained jumper that, asked to make a turn on an outside corner, braces his neck and makes for the stable.

Sometimes, after having gotten the horse under control, it may be necessary to circle him several times (a method known as "rolling-up") and get him confused before you can straighten him out. In this case, since the horse is resisting not from fear but from stubbornness, a good whack on the rump and a sharp application of the spur just as, in circling, you reach the point where you want him to head out, will often make up his mind for him and serve as a good lesson.

BOLTING

Bolting straight ahead either from fear or stubbornness is best controlled by a rein effect known as THE PULLEY REIN. Taking both reins up short, one in each hand, the rider grasps the mane half way up the neck at a point where the rein held in this hand

The stubborn horse that pops his shoulder out and runs out at an obstacle while keeping his head turned towards it. The correction is to take him in on a slight diagonal starting (in this case) to the left of the jump and heading him toward the right, straightening him on the final stride.

will be taut. Then, sitting deep in the saddle and throwing his weight back, he carries the other hand out away from the horse's neck and upward toward his own shoulder. The effect is to break up the resistance by tipping the muzzle of the horse sideward and upward, thus bringing the horse to a dead stop on a small circle.

This is a severe rein effect but is thoroughly effective, especially with animals which have developed the bolting habit as a vice. If you are riding with a pelham or Weymouth (full) bridle, keep the curb rein in the hand which you are raising and the other three in the hand braced on the horse's neck. Be sure that the reins in the bracing hand are taut as the horse will then be pulling against his own neck and will have to give in.

The animal that is bolting out of fear should be soothed. The obstinate one should be spoken to sharply and the rider should keep the reins short and ready to put into operation should he try the same thing again. As time goes on his lessons should include stopping short from a canter on the application of this rein effect until he learns that he cannot succeed in his attempts. In this training the rider should not be unduly rough unless the horse resists. The final test to prove the effectiveness of the training is to gallop the horse toward the stable and stop him on command without resistance.

THE BARN-RAT OR HERD BOUND HORSE

This is the animal which has never been properly taught to respond automatically to the aids. He will dive for the stable or refuse to leave it alone. He will dodge into the center of the ring or try to get out of the gate each time he passes it if working alone. He will refuse to leave his companions when, after working in company, the class lines up in the center and one horse at a time is asked to move out to the track and perform some specific exercise. This type of resistance is known to the British as "napping." It develops in insensitive animals either from very bad original training or from being ridden constantly by beginners. It is very common in ponies which are too small to have been correctly broken by an adult rider and, when turned over to a child who is incompetent, soon learn that they can do what they want.

The pulley-rein effect to correct the popping of the shoulder of the runaway. The rider's hand could be carried a little higher if the horse continues to resist.

The experienced rider can get on the determined barn-rat and with strong aids, including a sharp rap with the crop, manage him with no trouble. He can prevent the rogue which dives for the gate of the ring or the barn with a quick and uncomfortable use of the pulley rein described above. Unfortunately, this will not cure the animal. As soon as a less experienced rider mounts he will go back to his old tricks. He must return to the schooling arena and be taught to obey the aids automatically. When other horses are working in the ring with him he should work independently part of the time, circling out of line, riding in the opposite direction and passing, etc. One very good exercise is to have the problem horse turn and ride down the center line by himself while another rider turns from the opposite end and rides toward him. As the horses meet, both riders turn to their own right, thus turning the horses away from each other. The exercise is repeated several times, the riders turning first to their right, then to their left. A variation of this is for two riders, one on each long wall, to make circles which extend to the exact center of the ring. The two horses should meet on the center line and be made to continue their individual circles. This should be practiced first at the sitting trot and later at the canter. Any sign of resistance merits a sharp word and strong application of the legs. The rider should anticipate the resistance by being prepared and should use the aids *before* the horse actually tries to dodge out.

Bear in mind that the horse that bolts toward the barn or tries to run away when out on the trail from sheer stubbornness is rarely dangerous. He will take care of himself and therefore of his rider. The horse that bolts from fear is something else again, for he may become so hysterical that he will run "blind"—crossing a slippery road in traffic, crashing into a building, etc. The hysterical horse should be pulled up short with the pulley rein and kept only at a walk until you get him home. He should not be taken on the road alone again until he has lost his fear by riding in company and has learned confidence in his rider.

REARING

This is a vice which can be either the result of rough training

Diagram showing how in using the pulley-rein the muzzle of the horse is displaced to throw him off balance and break up the resistance. Care should be taken that he is always pulled toward the side on which he is leading at the canter, otherwise, since this is a very strong rein effect, he may fall.

As the riders meet they turn their horses' heads away from each other so that their mounts will be prepared to separate.

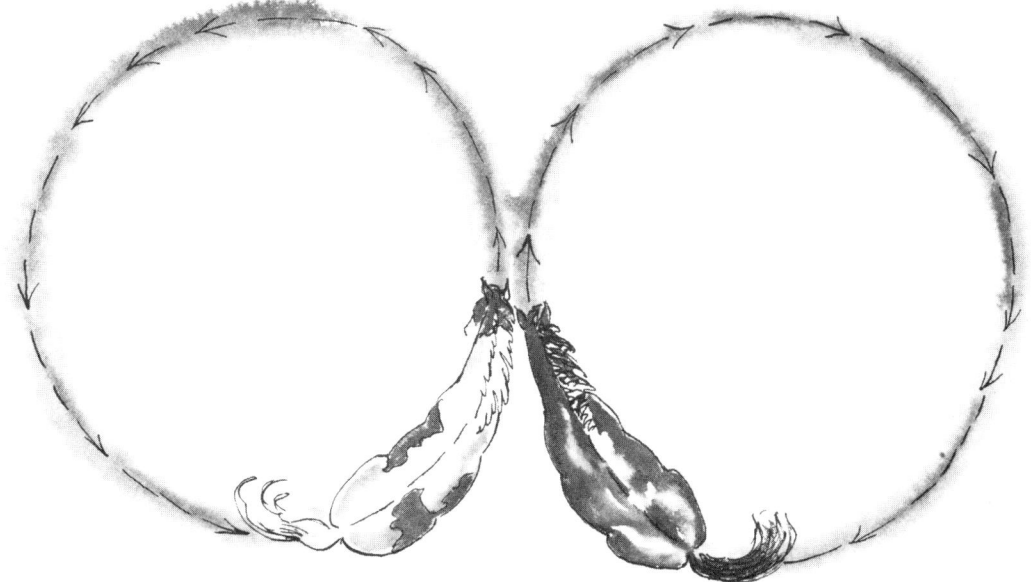

Riders riding in meeting circles to train herd-bound animals to be willing to leave each other.

or bad riding. Many horses rear in order to avoid doing something they don't want to do, such as entering the jumping arena, leaving the barn, passing through water, etc. The good rider will be able to handle the problem, but the poor rider will be helpless and should never be put on a horse that is known to have this vice for his instinctive reaction will be to hang on to the reins and let his weight come back. If the horse is not prepared for this, it may cause him to fall over backwards and a bad accident may occur. If the horse is in the air, the rider should throw his weight forward on his stirrups instead and hold on to the mane. As the horse comes down he should spur him on.

There is one method with which I have cured a number of horses that were rearing from vice. This is to put the horse in a situation which will encourage him to rear and, just before he goes up, slide the right-hand rein under the toe of the rider's boot, lean back and pull up on it. This brings the horse's nose to the boot and pins it there. He cannot possibly get off the ground in this position. At the same time the opposite leg should be used strongly to cause him to circle around and around. When he tries to stop, keep him going, still with his nose to the stirrup then, without warning, release the rein, straighten him out, and push him on. A few lessons of this sort will cure him of using this vice against any rider except an absolute beginner.

With the stubborn unexcitable horse whose rider is unable to use the method suggested, another cure (to be used only as a last resort) is usually very effective. The saddle should be taken off and a really good, athletic rider should mount. The horse is again tempted into rearing by putting him into a situation which is known to cause this response. As he goes up in the air the rider waits until he is at the top of his rear, then slides off to one side, and pulls the horse right over backwards! We broke a stubborn fourteen-hand pony which always refused to leave the barn or paddock alone and go to the schooling arena with this method. He had to be pulled over three times before he finally gave in but, once conquered, we had no more trouble.

THE BALKY HORSE

This is usually a cold-blooded animal that has never been

properly schooled. In the schooling ring he refuses to move out and, with a beginner, comes to a complete standstill. Asked to leave the line and cross the ring he will sometimes show his resistance, not by rearing or bolting but by backing up. A very good cure for this is to keep reining him back as rapidly as you can get him to move for a minimum of a hundred feet. Two or three such lessons should cure this particular vice. However, to teach him to move along readily he will have to go back to his early lessons and be taught to move out immediately on response to the aids. A sharp crack of the crop at the strategic instant will do a lot to straighten him out.

BUCKING

This is usually the type of resistance which is used by horses that have found they can remove their riders and so escape work by bucking. In young horses it is also sometimes simply the result of high spirits, too little work, cold weather, and too much oats. In any case, the rider must learn to feel when the buck is coming, sit tight, and keep the animal's head up. The young horse can usually be broken of this habit by the good rider and, in any case, will calm down and outgrow it. The confirmed bucker that deliberately takes advantage of the inexperienced rider should not be ridden except by those more capable and should receive a lot of schooling to teach him to obey the aids. If this doesn't work and he must be ridden by beginners he should be sent on his way.

THE HORSE THAT ATTEMPTS TO BRUSH THE RIDER OFF OR CROWD HIM AGAINST A WALL OR FENCE

This is rather a rare vice, but one does run into it occasionally. If the horse is used for hunting or cross-country work the rider should always be aware of the possibility of his horse attempting to take him under a low branch or knock his leg against the trunk of a tree. If he is alert he will feel the tensing of the horse's muscles under him and can stop him before he gets started. If he rides carelessly without paying attention he will have to duck suddenly or pull his leg up should the horse take him unawares. The horse that tries to crush the rider against the ring fence or the side of barn is easily controlled for the rider has only to keep the animal's head bent to the side in the direction of the proposed obstacle and the horse cannot possibly bring his body and the rider's leg against it.

RESTLESSNESS WHILE BEING MOUNTED

There are several forms of this. There is the horse that, as the rider prepares to put his foot into the stirrup, swings his quarters toward him and possibly tries to cow-kick. There are horses that swing their quarters away, horses that back up, move forward, or just dance up and down in place.

Let us take up each form of resistance in turn. In the case of the cow-kicker the rider stands well forward facing the rear. He takes up the reins very short with the rein toward him pulled tighter than the other so that the horse's head is bent to the left. He must keep tension on the reins all the time he is mounting and if he does this correctly the animal can neither swing his quarters toward him nor reach him if he tries to cow-kick.

For the animal that tries to swing his quarters away and thus prevent the rider from getting his foot into the stirrup, the opposite method is used. Here, standing facing the shoulder, the rider shortens the off rein so that the horse's head is bent to the right. The rider will then be able to mount with no trouble, provided he keeps tension on the reins.

If the horse has the habit of bolting forward the instant the rider puts his toe in the stirrup, the correction is again to have the reins tight but, in this case, even. The rider stands well forward and keeps strong contact on the bit. He mounts very slowly, putting his toe in the stirrup and pulling back with the reins if necessary to keep the horse from moving out. While going up he must still be ready to stop the horse should he move. When he is in the saddle he should make the animal stand at least a full minute before allowing him to move on.

For the horse that tries to avoid being mounted by backing up, the rider should stand well back and face forward, with his reins in contact. If the horse tries to back as he is raising his foot the

Mounting the horse that tries to cow-kick. To prevent this, the rider, mounting at the shoulder, bends the horse's head toward him.

Mounting the horse that tries to swing his haunches away. The rider now bends the horse's head to the right. Corrections of this kind are called "opposing the forehand to the haunches" since it is axiomatic that a horse cannot put his head and his quarters on the same spot at the same time.

rider gives him a sharp slap under the belly with the flat of his right hand.

The best cure for the horse with either of the last two confirmed habits of resistance to mounting or for the horse that is simply extremely restless is as follows. Supply yourself with a number of broken up bits of carrot. Taking the usual position for mounting, gather the reins, speak to the horse, and then offer him a bit of carrot. Now drop your reins and gather them again. Repeat the exercise twice more. The horse will now be programmed into waiting for the tidbit. Next put your foot in the stirrup but without resting any weight on it and, restraining the horse with the reins, quickly give him another tidbit. When the horse, after having been rewarded several times in this way, waits for his carrot, step up onto the stirrup but before swinging your leg across reach over and give him the carrot from the off side. Repeat the whole process with a tidbit at each step. Be sure the reins are always taut to prevent forward movement. On no account should you continue the process of mounting unless the horse remains absolutely immobile. No matter in what position you are, as he starts to move, take your left hand off his neck and pull back with the reins enough to halt the movement. The final step is to carry your leg well over his rump and settle lightly into the saddle, leaning forward with the final tidbit in your right hand as you do so. The horse should be kept standing for a moment after which you should dismount and repeat the lesson until your pupil is thoroughly trained. The next time you ride give him his carrot when you first gather up your reins and again after you are in the saddle, dispensing with the intermediate rewards.

The timid young horse or one which has been frightened by being mounted for the first time without sufficient preliminary training will be cured by the same method, although you will have to go much more slowly. For the first lesson it will be enough just to walk and stop every few steps. While he is halted you raise your foot about six inches from the ground and give him his tidbit. Continue this lesson for ten minutes or so, walking in both directions. Next day you will probably be able to get your foot as high as the stirrup—but without inserting it. Continue the lessons as described, teaching only one new step per day. It once took me five days to quiet the fears of a young Arabian stallion which I had bought. He was supposedly entirely untrained except for grooming and shoeing. He went through his lunging training calmly, learning rapidly, had no fear of the saddle, accepted the snaffle bit, etc. I was most surprised when he went up in the air with his eyes rolling in terror the first time I tried to mount him. There had been some teenaged boys at the stable where I bought him and I concluded that one of them must have jumped on his back unexpectedly and frightened him badly. As I said, it took five days but eventually he lost his fear and this was the only type of resistance I ever encountered in him.

In contrast, a dealer once dropped a horse off for me to look at. He seemed quiet enough but as I started to mount he kicked out and then tried to take off across the ring. He was evidently an old hand and had learned this resistance as the vice which would frighten many people and so save him from having to go to work. I went for my supply of carrots and in fifteen minutes he would stand still with the reins loose.

STALL COURAGE

Many horses become nervous and excitable due to natural high spirits, good condition, lack of exercise, over-feeding of grain, and/or cold temperatures. Animals which, in summer, are perfectly calm under the most inept beginner will take to bucking unexpectedly, sidling across the paddock or along the trail, and blowing through distended nostrils as though they expected to find a sabretoothed tiger behind every bush as soon as the temperature drops.

The most successful method of remedying this problem is to turn the animal out in a paddock or schooling arena before he is saddled up. After he has had the usual roll to scratch his back he should be encouraged to play, buck, and fling his heels to the sky. It is generally even more satisfactory if several horses can be put out together, since they will run each other around for ten or fifteen minutes. When they stop playing of their own accord, sniff the ground, scratch each other's withers, or just stand quietly resting on three legs they may be brought in, brushed off and saddled up. They will then usually be perfectly quiet even under a poor rider. This method is much more effective than that of

Training the horse to stand by mounting, giving the animal a tidbit at each stage.

lunging or riding the horse to quiet him down.

It should also be remembered that whenever a horse has to be kept in his stall for a day his grain ration should be cut in half.

ROLLING IN THE SADDLE

Some horses and ponies like to roll in the saddle while being ridden. This is not for the purpose of getting the rider off but merely shows that they want to scratch their backs or relax in a tempting mudpuddle or stream on a hot day. I have found that an animal suffering from this compulsion will be much less apt to try it if, like the horse with stall courage, he is turned into the arena for a few minutes before being saddled. There he is allowed to roll to his heart's content. However, all riders should be warned of his propensity and should take up a short rein in crossing ploughed fields, puddles, or water, using their legs or crop immediately if the horse starts to paw or buckle at the knees preparatory to going down.

TOSSING THE HEAD

This habit comes from nervousness, fatigue, or as an effort to escape the bit. The best solution is to ride the horse for awhile on side reins as described on pages 64–65. For the horse that resists by hanging on the bit or which tries to eat grass while being ridden, a check rein as advised on page 40 can be devised. Eating grass can also be prevented by putting a leather muzzle on the animal.

ABOVE THE BIT

We have recommended reins and exercises to teach flexion of the poll for the star-gazer. For the horse that does not stargaze but tries to get above the bit by carrying his head too high and that does not engage his hindquarters and reach out with his forelegs on a strong trot, circles with the haunches ranged out will be found effective. The horse is ridden at the sitting trot in a circle or volt about ten or twelve feet in diameter. After he is going quietly, the rider pushes the haunches off the track to the outside, using his inside leg behind the girth. It is only necessary for the haunches to be displaced from six inches to a foot. Because his hindquarters will now have to execute a larger circle than his forehand, the horse will react by dropping his head and throwing his center of gravity forward. In extreme cases, it may be necessary to ride such a horse with draw reins. This is a type of rein which has a loop through which the front billet strap is slipped. The rein then comes through the snaffle ring to the rider's hand. Another way of rigging it, which is more severe, is to attach it to the girth at the brisket. Great care should be used with such appliances as it is easy to over-flex the horse or cause him to bend his neck half way down to the withers instead of at the poll.

BITS AND BITTING

Many problems with head carriage, resistance against the bit, and flexion of the gullet, jaw, and poll are related to the types of bits used and the methods used in getting the horse accustomed to the feel of the bit in his mouth. The three most common types of bits are the snaffle, the pelham, and the Weymouth or full bridle. There is also the Kimberwick and a special type called a "three-in-one" bit which is manufactured in England. Let us discuss these different types and their uses.

The snaffle is the familiar bit with a jointed mouthpiece and circular rings or rings shaped like d's to which the reins are fastened. There is a school which believes that good riders use only snaffles as this shows that they do not need a more severe bit to control their horse. Used with a running martingale, the snaffle is the most popular bit for hunting and stadium jumping, since should the rider come back on his horse's mouth due to being taken unawares and left behind, the horse does not suffer as much as he would if bitted with a pelham or Weymouth.

All young horses are given their basic training in snaffles. However, the fact is that it takes more sensitive and educated hands to ride in a Weymouth or pelham than in a snaffle. The beginner cannot haul away on the horse's mouth to maintain his balance since the horse will resent it and become restive or refuse to move out. In advanced dressage, there are certain rein

Horse with head too high, stiff poll.

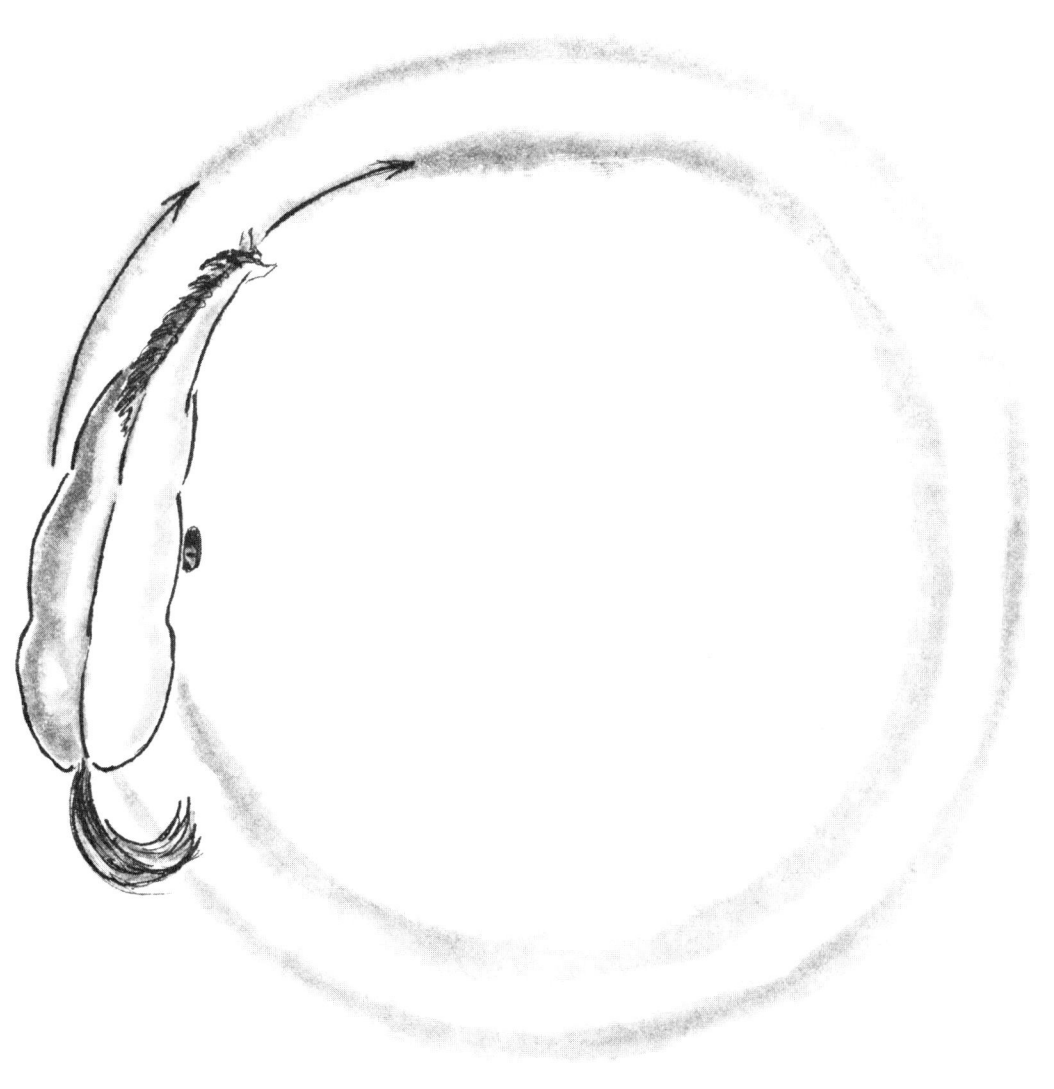

Correction by riding in circles with the haunches ranged out.

effects which can be obtained with four reins which cannot be obtained with two. In all my life I have ridden only one horse which I preferred to ride in a snaffle. This was Mr. X mentioned before. His mouth was like silk. He could be going at a full gallop in the hunt field and would pull in to a walk or halt with a motion from my little finger.

At the Spanish Riding School in Vienna, the young horse learns all his basic and intermediate dressage training in a snaffle. He is then ridden in a Weymouth, the reins of the snaffle and those of the curb being held with equal tension. When his schooling is considered to be at its most advanced stage the rider uses the curb rein only; the snaffle hangs in loops to show that the horse is so well trained and the hands of the rider so sensitive that he will go through all the figures on the curb with no sign of discomfort, resistance, or nervousness. When riding in this way, the reins are held in one hand and the rider carries a crop vertically in the other with the handle pointing downward and its tip up.

I have hunted for five seasons in Ireland where every horse is fitted with a snaffle and to use anything else is considered a disgrace. I always took my own saddle (the Irish saddles with which the "hirelings" are provided are terribly uncomfortable) and I also took my own pelham bridle. The first time I appeared so equipped the owner of the stable looked horror-stricken. He held the bridle up at arm's length as though it were a venomous serpent about to bite him.

"Surely, Madam, you'll never be wanting to put the likes of this in my poor horse's mouth, would you now? Why, you could pull a horse over backwards with such a contraption and break his back!"

"I certainly won't use it if I can hold him in a snaffle," I told him. "I tell you what we'll do. My taxi will follow the hunt, I understand. I'll put the bridle in that. If at the end of the first run I find I don't need it, I won't put it on the horse. But I've no intention of over-running hounds or getting ahead of the Master and Hunt Staff. And I assure you I won't pull your horse over backwards or jab him in the mouth."

He looked a little dubious but, as he planned to go along on the hunt himself, he evidently felt he could keep an eye on me. Sure enough, the horse was very strong with a hard mouth and after the first run I changed bridles. The owner, by now, realized that I knew what I was doing and made no demur. Word must have been passed around from one hunt to another for no one ever again objected when I produced my bridle. In fact, on one hunt, the owner was extremely surprised when I brought in a rather nervous, sensitive horse, cool and at a long reined walk. He told me that never before had the horse come back from the hunt except in a heavy sweat and dancing every step of the way.

In our school, all beginning riders ride for a little while in hackamores. When they have got their balance, both with and without stirrups, they are permitted bridles and use whatever type the horse or pony is accustomed to. Later, when they start jumping, they go back to the hackamore until they no longer come back over the jumps and are skillful enough so that, if the horse takes off a little too far from the jump and the rider is left behind he can drop his reins entirely to avoid hurting his horse's mouth.

The pelham is a curb-type bit with or without a port in the mouthpiece to take pressure off the tongue and with two pairs of rings; one for snaffle reins and the other for curb reins. Many people say that the snaffle does not actually work like a snaffle but like a modified curb and that the bit is badly designed. My own experience has been that there are many horses which go quietly in a pelham but are nervous in a full bridle or Weymouth. There are several varieties of pelhams: jointed pelhams, mullein mouthed (those with a curved mouthpiece but no port), rubber pelhams, Tom Thumbs, etc. And there are many different lengths of cheekpieces and types of ports from which to choose.

The Kimberwick is a pelham with the shank cut off just below the snaffle ring. It has a mouthpiece with a low port and a curb chain, but only one pair of reins. It is useful for the horse that is too strong going in a snaffle but is nervous in an ordinary pelham or in a double bridle. It is also useful for riders who need to learn not to lean on the bit and who are unaccustomed to handling four reins.

The three-in-one bit is one of the most interesting and practical bits I have ever run across. This year I have been schooling a very sensitive thirteen-year-old horse that had been ridden with heavy hands and too strong legs. He was so hysterical as a result that he had an upside-down neck, no flexion of poll or jaw at all, no engagement of the haunches, could not extend his head, put his weight on his forehand and could therefore take only choppy little steps, was so stiff in his body and all his joints that his gaits jolted the rider terribly, and he could not bend at all laterally, not even in the neck. He had been ridden in a snaffle with a running martingale. I rode him for six weeks in a hackamore, got him to relax, to extend, to bend, and to use his loins. He also learned to flex at the poll and his head carriage was good, but I could not teach him to relax his jaw and come up under me in stopping. In the snaffle he opened his mouth. I tried a dropped nose band. This prevented him from opening his mouth but now he began to bore. He combined the two resistances when ridden in a Weymouth. There was no ordinary pelham available—and then a friend introduced me to the three-in-one. This bit is of a completely different design. What would normally be the curb has a mouthpiece and lower rings for the reins but no loop at the top for the cheek straps. Instead the upper ends of the cheeks (shanks) are in the form of a corkscrew spiral. On the mouthpiece there are two loose rings like the ordinary round rings of the snaffle bridle but instead of being fixed they slide back and forth along the mouthpiece and are so designed that they cannot go around. It is to these that the cheek straps of the bridle fasten. The shanks of the curb are short, about the length of those of the Tom Thumb, and because they are not fastened to the cheek straps there is much more play and movement when the reins are used. The curb chain is run through the snaffle rings from behind and hooked over the spirals which form the free moving ends of the curb bit. When the snaffle reins are used alone the curb chain is not engaged so the action is truly that of a snaffle.

The horse with which I have been working goes perfectly in this bit. He can be controlled with a touch, flexes beautifully, is willing to drop his head and lean on it for the extended gaits, yet keeps his mouth closed and gives as soon as either rein is used.

Bitting

Many problems relating to acceptance of the bit, flexion, and head carriage can be avoided if the horse is introduced to the bit in such a way as to make him like it. Our young horses are first schooled on the longe with a regular schooling cavesson. When the time comes to introduce him to the snaffle bit, the colt is backed into a standing stall and cross-tied or he is cross-tied in the open upper half of his box stall. The snaffle is rubbed with molasses before being put in his mouth and it is adjusted to hang quite low on the tongue but not so low that the colt can get his tongue over it. The chains or halter shanks by which he is tied give him plenty of room to raise and lower his head.

All colts start by chewing the bit. When they are introduced to it in this way there is no pressure on bars or lips, the colt likes the taste, and he also likes to play with it, snatching at it and in doing so, flexing at the poll. I have found that this preliminary training, which lasts until the animal accepts the feel of the bit and no longer tries to snatch at it, saves days and weeks of trying to get him used to the feeling of it in his mouth.

The next step is the usual one of schooling him with the snaffle on under the cavesson and with long side reins attached. When we first start riding him it is in the hackamore with the snaffle under it.

Using this method, no young horse that I have ever trained has developed anything other than a perfect mouth and head carriage. Many have served in the school under all kinds of riders for from ten to twenty or more years, and they remained sensitive and obedient with no resistances, such as boring or star-gazing until the day they had to be put down.

PROBLEMS IN THE STABLE

Few horses nowadays give trouble in the stable since most are so well handled as foals that they never build up any type of resistance. However, once in a while one runs across a horse with one or more of the following problems.

Crowding in the Stall

This used to be common when more horses were stabled in standing or straight stalls. The animal would wait until a man entered the stall and then would try to crush him against the side by crowding him with his body. The remedy is to provide oneself with a piece of two-by-four, the ends of which have been sharpened to dull points. This implement should be a few inches longer than the width of your body so that the points protude when it is held horizonally in front of you just above your hips. If the horse tries to crowd when you enter the stall thus armed, he will come up against the point of the two-by-four with his own body while the opposite point can be held steady against the wall.

Kicking the Side of the Stall

This is a common vice with high strung horses or with those which get over-excited while waiting to be fed. The cure is to attach an eighteen-inch length of hat elastic to a rubber ball and tie the elastic around the horse's back leg above the hock. Usually only one ball is necessary, but you may have to use two balls with two elastics and put them on both back legs. When the horse kicks the balls fly out and hit him on the cannon bone.

Cribbing and Sucking Wind

This is one of the most pernicious and difficult habits to break. The horse grabs the edge of his manger, water bucket, partition, or stall door and bites, at the same time grunting in a specific fashion. The common treatment is to keep a "cribbing strap" on the horse at all times except when he is being ridden. This strap, which fits tight at the throttle, prevents the horse from distending the muscles at the throttle but does not prevent him from chewing on the tempting surfaces. No one knows what the cause of this habit is, but if it is not halted as soon as discovered it becomes compulsory. We once had two young colts who started to chew wood because they were kept in a small paddock and were bored. They would probably have gone on to wind sucking but we turned them out in the big pasture with the herd and they forgot about it.

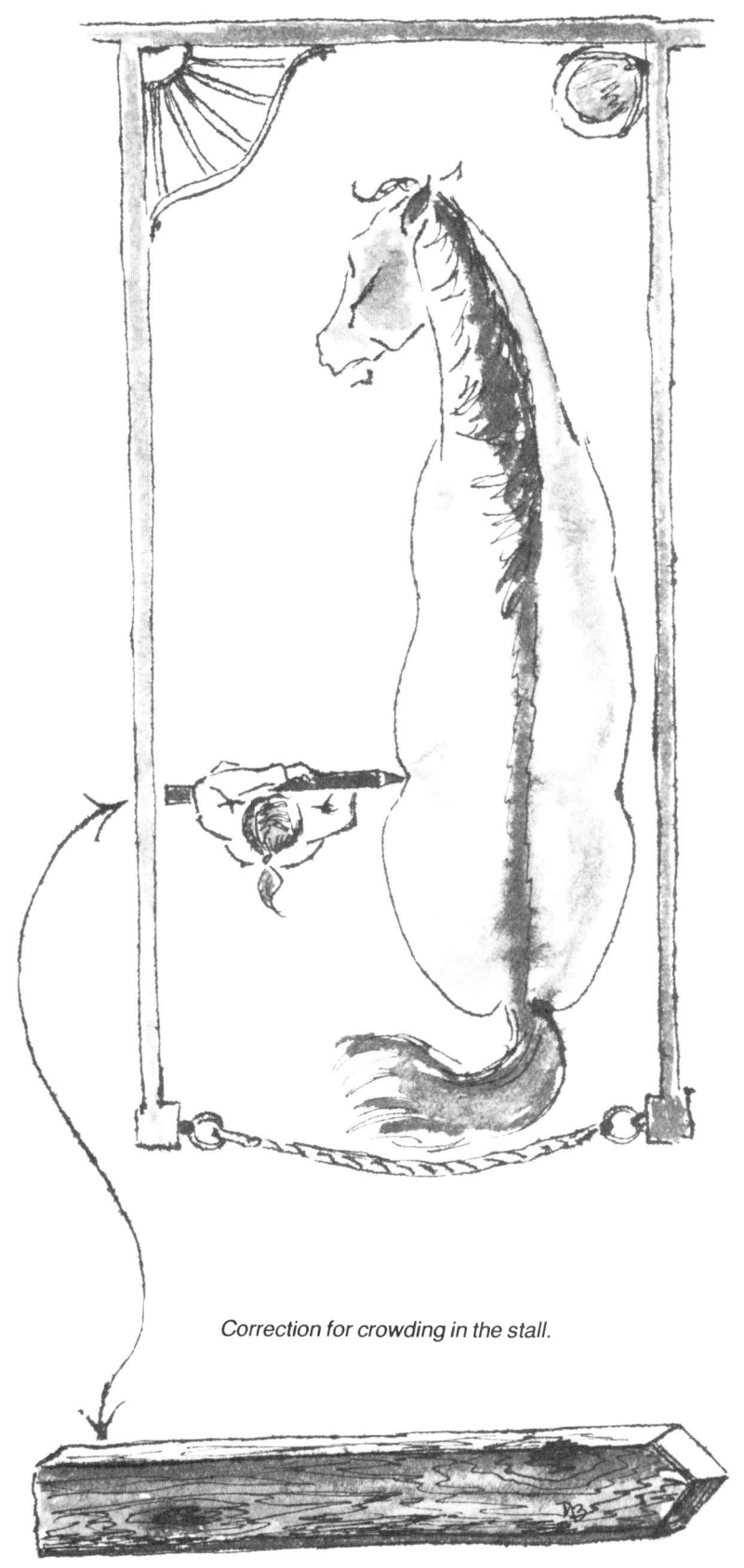

Correction for crowding in the stall.

Correction for the horse that kicks the side of his stall.

HALTER BREAKING AND LEADING

The only time in the whole training period when the horse *should* show resistance is in his very first lesson of learning to accept the halter and to follow on a leading shank or stand tied without pulling back. The trainer should make these early lessons as easy as possible. In the first few days of the foal's life the halter is put on and fitted so that is comfortable. Meanwhile, he is handled all over every day and his confidence is gained so that the appearance of a human being in the stall is not a frightening one. Now comes the time when he must learn the "lesson of the rope." We use the following procedure.

Next to the manger of the mare and about 2½ feet above the stall floor we put a very large screw eye. We then rig up a halter shank with a block of wood at one end and a snap at the other. This is run through the screw eye from below so that the block of wood hangs down. It should be of such a length that when the snap is fastened to the foal's halter the block just touches the ground.

The mare is now tied in the stall to the ring over her manger and the baby is brought up beside her and the snap fastened to his halter. He will be able to back up the length of the rope but when the block hits the screw eye he will be halted. The trainer should be at hand standing right behind the foal. At first the foal will not realize that he is tied, but then he will back up or turn and come up against the resistance. His first reaction will be to pull back. As long as he doesn't get to struggling hysterically or trying to throw himself backwards the trainer should not interfere. If the foal gets too excited the trainer should come up to him from behind, brace his body aganist the haunches of the foal and gently push him forward: the tension on the shank will be released and the foal will stop struggling. After two or three tries he will finally begin to connect cause and effect and it won't be too long before he stops trying to pull away. He should never be left tied up alone until the trainer is perfectly sure that he understands this.

Now we come to training the foal to lead. Two people are needed, one to lead the mare, the other the foal. He will follow willingly but should be checked if he tries to run ahead. When he

The right way to train a foal not to resist the rope.

has learned this lesson, the person leading the mare walks her ahead ten feet or so and stops her while the one who is handling the foal holds the latter back. He is then allowed to catch up to her but must do so at a walk, not at a wild dash.

The hardest lesson is for the foal to learn to follow the pull of the shank when it takes him ahead of or away from the mare. It may be necessary for a third person to come up behind and boost the little fellow along. If there is no assistant, the halter shank can be carried around the tiny haunches and the foal pulled along in this fashion. However, it will be necessary to grasp both the free end and the end about eight inches from the snap so that the rope is pulled without pulling back on the halter.

If a horse that is well halter broken does not want to follow for some reason, do not look back at him but swing his forehand a step to one side and then to the other. This will break up his resistance and he will follow.

PROBLEMS WITH CLIPPING

Many horses are terrified of the clippers, especially when they are used around the head. It is often necessary to use a twitch, and it is better to do so than to risk having the horse hurt himself in his efforts to get away. I am told that horses accustomed to being groomed with a horse vacuum are never afraid of clippers. If one were to get the young foal or the horse that is badly frightened by the sound of the clippers used to it by hanging a set in the stall or just outside it and then letting them run for several hours a day it might help. The next step would be to turn the clippers upside down and run them all over the less sensitive parts of the body without cutting with them. After this would come the regular use of them, starting with the withers, upper legs, and body, and gradually approaching the neck and head. With a very nervous horse a tranquilizer given by the veterinarian may help to some extent, although I have handled certain horses that were so terrified that they had to be completely anesthetized. Usually the twitch will work and need be used only when the horse becomes restless as the machine approaches his head and legs.

Teaching the foal to lead by means of a halter shank around his haunches.

VANNING

Twenty-five or thirty years ago most horses were afraid of being vanned. Now that there is so much interest in showing and there are so many local shows the average horse has been trained out of this as a foal.

The primary fear is that of being loaded. The ramp is of different material than the ground or the stable floor and it is not perfectly steady. If the foal has been taught to follow over such unusual footing there will be no problem, but if not, there are several methods whereby the reluctant animal can be loaded successfully.

First, there is the method employing a two-by-four eight feet long. The horse is led toward the ramp at a walk, and as he approaches it two men carrying the bar at a height slightly above that of the horse's hocks come up behind him. Because of the position of his eyes the horse can see the approaching bar and, nine times out of ten, he will continue quietly up the ramp. This method will only work if there are side rails to the ramp.

The second method is the rope method. This is more practical than the two-by-four method if there are no side railings. A twenty-foot rope is attached to each side of the doorway leading into the van. If there are side rails to the ramp the ropes can be attached to the ends of those. One assistant takes hold of the free end of each rope. They form an aisle with the ropes and the horse is led between them. As he passes them, the two assistants change sides so that the ropes cross and are held taut against the horse's hindquarters. By shortening the ropes and moving toward the van as the horse advances the assistants can literally shove him up the ramp.

When using either of the these methods the person leading the animal must be careful not to walk directly in front of him since, on stepping on the ramp and feeling the insecurity of it, the horse will sometimes jump from the end of it into the van.

Sometimes a very timid horse will come right up to the ramp, as pushed by the ropes, and will then balk. Two more people will now be needed—one to stand beside each front leg. First one of the horse's feet is lifted and placed on the ramp. The person on the opposite side now leans his shoulder against that of the horse

Loading an unwilling horse by coming up behind him with a two-by-four.

Using ropes to urge an unwilling horse into a van.

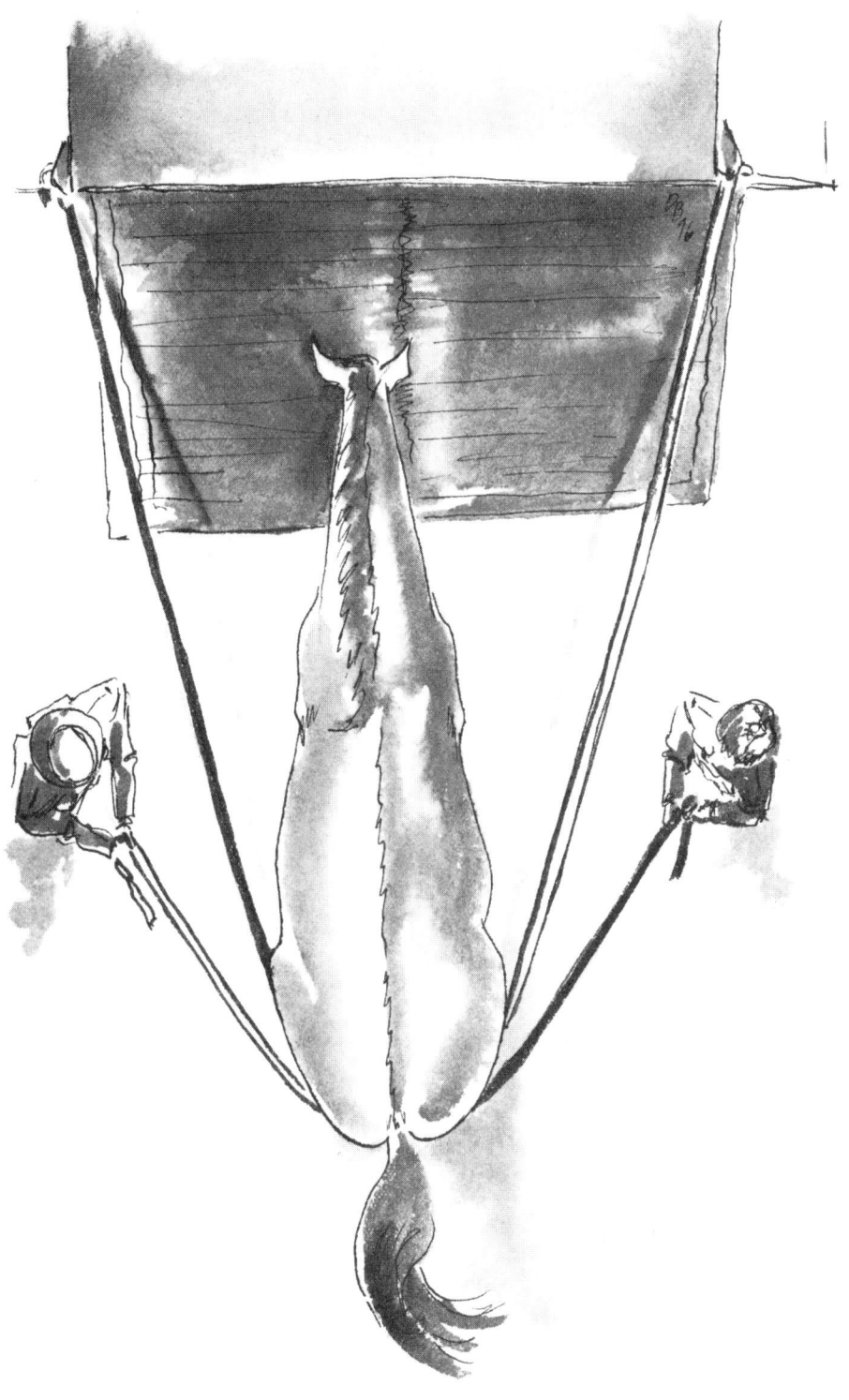

Diagram showing how assistants stand and how the ropes are maneuvered.

and lifts the foot on that side. As soon as it is down the other man brings his weight to bear on the shoulder on his side and picks up that front foot and advances it another step, etc. When he finds that the footing does not give way the horse will usually walk the rest of the way, but we once owned a Saddlebred named Colonel who had to have a man on each of his four feet and be "walked" the length of the ramp every time he was loaded!

CONTROLLING THE NERVOUS HORSE FOR MEDICATION

Many horses are restless when they must be treated for wounds, abrasions, or any injury around the head. This may also apply to having their teeth floated. In difficult cases a twitch may have to be used. Tranquilizers will also help. For less nervous animals it may only be necessary for an assistant to hold up one foreleg. In giving an injection the veterinarian will often slap the area to be injected several times and then thrust the needle in quickly. Even a nervous horse never notices the difference between the slap and the prick of the needle. If the treatment will take some time, such as putting on a poultice or soaking a sprained tendon in Epsom salts, an assistant standing at the horse's head can hold a pan of oats under his nose and let him keep munching. Loud noises and sudden movements should be avoided and everything should be done to convince the horse that there is no need for fear.

CATCHING THE HORSE IN THE FIELD

Most horses will come readily up to be caught. Occasionally one runs across an animal which has been frightened or which has never had enough handling to permit this. One way to take care of the situation is to get the horse to follow you as you walk ahead rattling grain in a pail. Another way is to approach as closely as you can, then kneel and take a handful of grass and rub it between the palms of your hands so that it rustles. Many horses or ponies, overcome with curiosity, will come up and reach a nose out to see what you have. Needless to say you should move your hand very quietly and slowly in reaching up for the halter. Some animals will allow themselves to be caught if the owner does not carry a halter shank, and will pull away if an attempt is made to lead them without the shank. A leather belt buckled around your waist and slipped off after your have your hand around the animal's neck will take the place of the shank and can even be used instead of a halter if necessary. It should be looped over the poll just in back of the ears and held tightly under the throttle.

As a last resort the animal can be herded into a corner. Two people with a twenty-foot rope can then pin the animal in the corner by following the two walls or fences which form the corner until they have the rope against the body of the horse. The man nearest the head will then be able to take hold of the halter. If the horse wears no halter and is very frightened, a third person should approach quietly with a tidbit and gradually calm him down until he is able to slip the halter on while the men with the ropes keep the tension.

Horses known to be very difficult to catch in the pasture or very headshy should be turned out with a two-foot halter shank attached so that in catching them it will not be necessary to raise a hand up to the head. As with everything else, when a horse is resisting from fear, every effort should be made to get his confidence rather than to frighten him and so create two fears where there was only one before.

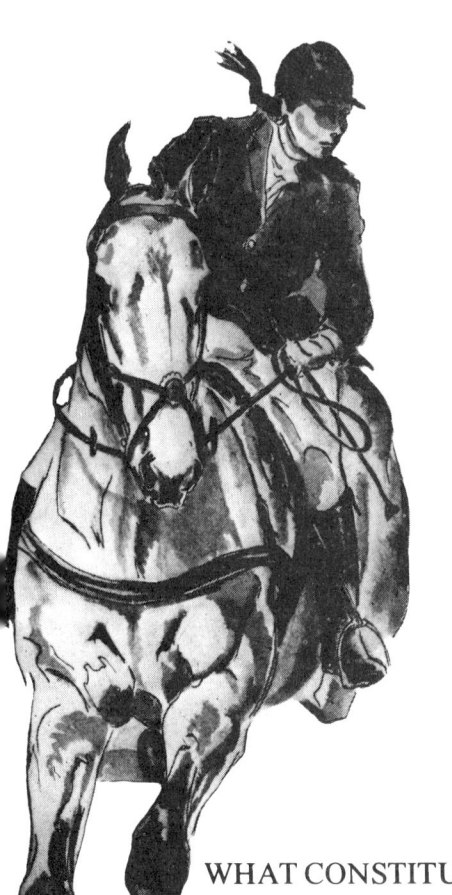

V

The Problem Horseman

WHAT CONSTITUTES A PROBLEM HORSEMAN?

We have discussed the problems which riders meet when working with various types of horses. What about the different kinds of riders with whom the horse must cope? Which of these could be called "problem horsemen"?

Let us look at the matter from the horse's point of view. To the untrained horse, *all* riders are problems. The horse must learn to understand what the rider wants him to do and then become disciplined into willingly obeying to the extent that his physical and mental capabilities permit. Until he has learned exactly what is wanted of him, the horse cannot learn to obey. Obviously, the rider of such a horse must be so experienced that he cannot only manage a green and inexperienced animal, but also knows how to enlarge the horse's knowledge and improve him. Anyone undertaking such a task without this necessary experience and skill faces defeat and failure, since to his horse he will be an unsolvable problem, while the horse will become increasingly resistant to him.

Now we come to the horse that has had the ordinary basic training. He will not find his rider a problem, provided that the rider's skill and demands are equal to those skills the horse has learned. Since a docile and somewhat lethargic horse is less easily upset by unskillful handling, such a horse is more suited to the needs of the intermediate rider than is the more highly trained one which has been taught to obey "the wind from the rider's spur."

To the horse that is wise in the ways of the beginner and has learned to take advantage of the totally inexperienced rider, the rider will present no problem since the horse will speedily get his own way and it is the rider who will suffer. Needless to say, when an experienced horseman gets on the erstwhile stubborn, disobedient animal, the outlaw obeys immediately—to the surprise of the beginner who cannot see that any methods other than those he thought he was employing are being used.

We have been speaking only from the point of view of the average horse. When the real "problem horse" as described earlier encounters the problem rider, the result can only be chaos and both will suffer.

WHAT LEADS TO THE DEVELOPMENT OF A PROBLEM RIDER?

There are some people who ride for a lifetime, yet never get beyond the "beginner" stage, and who will always be regarded as "problems" by all except the most docile of horses. The cause of this is the failure of the rider to realize that the horse is an individual with a mentality all its own, and that no two horses are alike in their reactions. Instead, the inexperienced person about to embark on his career as a horseman thinks of his mount as a mechanical creature. One has only to learn to "push the right button" and the horse will always and automatically react the way he is supposed to.

It takes only a few minutes in the saddle for the sensitive beginner to learn that this is not so. If he then goes to some reputable stable where he can get good instruction, he eventually develops skill enough to manage a suitable animal. He will probably ride in a group at first, since horses, being herd creatures, work best in company. After some months he will begin to feel very capable. His horse now starts, stops, turns, and takes up the various gaits on demand. He can sit correctly and is comfortable, but he has much more to learn before he can be considered an experienced horseman.

The Horse as Instructor

If the stable where such a rider is taking instruction is conscientious, once he has reached this stage he will be given the opportunity to ride many different horses, although these will still be carefully selected so that they are not too highly schooled or too sensitive, and do not have bad habits with which he cannot yet cope. Some stables, however, are more interested in keeping their pupils happy and satisfied than in teaching them, and will let them ride the same animal time after time. Since the horse is the real teacher, this is like letting a child study under just one master who is proficient in only one subject and to continue doing so throughout his school years.

Or, having fallen in love with one horse, the rider may buy him thinking that by owning a horse and so having unlimited opportunity to practice, he will soon become expert. This quite often happens with young people who, after a year or so at a riding school, persuade their parents to buy them a pony. Yet the day will surely come when, invited to ride a friend's animal and positive of his own skill, such a young rider will discover that he is far from being the master horseman he thought himself to be.

The Timid Rider

The timid rider who has little self-confidence will never be able to ride any animal other than an extremely docile one until, through experience, he has lost his timidity. Many girls and boys under ten or twelve start out by being very timid, but with proper instruction and suitable mounts, they often lose all their fears. Women who are timid by nature, and who take up riding after the age of 18 or 20, rarely lose their timidity entirely. This does not mean that they cannot enjoy themselves on the trail or in the ring, but they should never attempt to reschool a difficult horse or ride a highly sensitive animal.

The Over-Bold Rider

The overconfident person with limited experience should not attempt to ride a problem horse either. Such a rider, in all probability, is convinced that all horses can be conquered by strong hands and legs. A sensitive horse will be driven wild by such methods and a surly, hard-mouthed beast will only become more so.

THE HORSEMAN'S GOAL

What must the rider starting his career, or the one who may have ridden for many years but still feels that there is much to learn if he is to become truly expert, envisage as a goal? Xenophon the Greek, who lived about 400 B.C., wrote several books on equestrian subjects, one of which was on riding and training the horse. As his frontispiece he chose a drawing of a centaur, thus expressing every horseman's goal to become one with his horse so that the two act as harmoniously and automatically as though one brain were commanding and one system of muscles and nerves were obeying that brain, creating a single body. The brain of the man commands, to be clearly understood by the limbs and body of the horse and obeyed instantly. In turn, the brain of the man knows what every part of the horse's body is doing.

To achieve this goal at least partially, the horseman must develop three skills. Each of these is used in a prescribed sequence at every stage of training both the horse and the rider and in every situation which may occur while the rider is mounted.

These skills, stated many times by many authorities, are as follows. *First* the rider FEELS what the horse under him is doing or is about to do; *second*, he INTERPRETS what he feels; and *finally*, he either INFLUENCES the actions of his horse by using his aids or he remains passive.

The most important and essential of these skills is that of developing sensitivity to feel. The first time he mounts his horse any beginner can immediately feel and interpret the movement of starting and stopping. Next he learns to feel and interpret the difference between the trot and the canter. He can also feel

The Centaur, the Greek idea of the master rider.

when a horse stumbles badly under him or swerves with fright.

The real horseman has a much more highly developed sense of feeling. At the canter, he knows on which lead the horse is moving without looking at the horse's shoulder. In turning he knows whether the horse is bending his spine correctly so that the tracks of the hind feet follow the path of those of the front. In performing a volt or a circle he knows if the figure is perfectly round, if the horse executes it while maintaining the proper curvature, if the haunches are being used correctly, and he feels at once if the circle tends to be larger on one side than on the other, or is not centered at a specific spot, or if the horse is trying to make it smaller or larger.

Riding on straight lines, the rider feels when the horse is *about to* lengthen or shorten his strides, increase or decrease the cadence, or break the gait. This knowledge comes to the rider in plenty of time for him to interpret what he feels and influence the horse accordingly.

If, in riding at the trot, there is some slight deviation in stride, the experienced horseman will know which leg is affected. In approaching a jump, he can feel the horse prepare to gather himself for the take-off. On the trail he senses, by the way the horse moves, any symptom of fear.

DEVELOPING THE ABILITY TO FEEL

Before the rider can hope to learn to feel what the horse is doing or preparing to do he must learn to ride completely relaxed and to be independent of using his hands or his legs to stay on his horse. He must be as much at home without his reins and stirrups as with them. To accomplish this, he must learn to depend on a correct seat which puts his center of gravity over his stirrups and in line with that of his horse.

A simple demonstration of this balance can be done as follows: Sit on a stool in the normal manner with your weight on your buttocks and your feet apart as though they were in stirrups but too far in front of you. If someone joggles the stool roughly or pulls it out from under you, you will fall. Now bring your feet back on either side of the stool so that your ankles are in line with your hips. If someone pulls the stool out from under you when you are sitting this way, by simply putting your weight on your feet you will not fall. An old admonition used to be, "sit in your saddle as though you were standing on the ground with your knees bent and the horse came in under you."

This position of the legs is important in other ways. Unless the rider keeps his legs and feet perfectly still instead of swinging them back and forth under him in his efforts to rise to the posting trot as most beginners do, the sensitive horse will be disturbed. The old school horse will know at once that his rider is not experienced and may take advantage of that knowledge.

However, just sitting in the correct position is not enough. The rider must be completely relaxed so that the movements of his own body, especially of his loins and lower spine, will permit him to stay in contact with the saddle. It should also be remembered that the instant he stiffens any muscle in his thighs, calves, shoulders, or arms he loses his ability to feel. Furthermore, the horse knows at once when the rider stiffens and, according to his own temperament and training, he will react.

Except when the rider purposely comes forward and raises his buttocks out of the saddle in order to take the weight of the horse's loins and put it on his shoulders, as well as in the "up" position at the posting trot, the two "sitting bones" (lower points of the pelvis) should always remain in contact with the saddle or with the horse's back if the rider is riding without a saddle. This is particularly hard to do when riding at the sitting trot with a saddle or when learning to follow the movements of the canter.

It is necessary to understand why the sitting trot is so difficult, and why relaxed muscles are a must. Think of a person holding a ping-pong racquet. On the racquet is a hard ping-pong ball. If the racquet is suddenly lowered a foot or so but kept level, the ball will not stay with the racquet. The racquet will drop away and the ball will come down on it an instant later and will bounce. However, if a sponge is placed on the racquet, the sponge will follow the movement of the racquet. If the sponge or a completely deflated ball is dropped on the floor, it will not bounce as does the ping-pong ball.

Now let us see what happens when the horse trots. Since the trot is a diagonal gait, the horse is flexing his diagonal leg joints

The person on the left has been sitting on a stool in the normal way with her feet in front of her. Result—when the stool breaks or is pulled out from under her she lands on the ground.

In this drawing she has been sitting as one does on a horse with her weight balanced over her feet. When the stool is pulled away she has only to straighten her knees slightly and she will remain standing on the ground instead of falling.

Posting, correctly and incorrectly. This is a profile of two figures, one showing the swinging of the leg and the bouncing up and down of the hand as the rider, behind in the saddle, posts. The other shows a steady hand and leg.

in unison. If you watch the movement in slow motion on a film you will see that each time he flexes his legs his whole body drops several inches, only to immediately rise and drop again when the other pair of diagonal legs is raised. It is this drop of the body that the rider must learn to stay with, as though he were the soft sponge and not the hard ping-pong ball. He does this by keeping his muscles soft and relaxed and also by stretching his loins and pushing deep into the saddle at each step.

The movement is much easier to learn if the rider practices without his stirrups, preferably on a saddle pad rather than on a slippery saddle. Working in a ring following another horse which maintains a steady, even pace, or working in a long line is also helpful.

Many instructors feel it is important that, when riding without stirrups, the rider learn to keep a "fixed leg" position from the beginning. This is certainly the ultimate goal but, with a beginner, the purpose of the exercise is to teach relaxation and use of the loins in order to maintain contact with the saddle or the horse at the sitting trot. Introducing the fixed leg at this point will prevent attainment of this goal since no rider can learn the fixed leg and still not squeeze his thigh muscles unless he has first learned to sit relaxed and deep in his saddle. Having learned that, he can then progress to practicing the fixed leg (knee bent, ankle flexed, and heel lower than the toe).

He first learns the correct leg and foot position in his stirrups, and practices it constantly while the horse is standing and while he is moving. It is not difficult to place the leg in the correct position while the horse is standing but it is hard to learn to keep it there while posting or at the canter. As explained earlier, the tendency is for the leg to swing forward as the rider sits down and to swing back again as he rises. The exercise to correct this is for the rider to put both hands on his waist while at the halt, and to post up and down while the instructor or another rider watches to be sure that the legs remain steady. It may even be necessary for someone to hold his foot still. The exercise will be impossible if the rider's feet are not under him where they belong. The next step is to practice at a walk, maintaining the "up" or balanced position for several steps before settling down again. Care must be taken that the rider does not *stand up* in his

The ball that is highly inflated bounces when dropped. The partially inflated ball does not do so. The rider that tightens his thigh muscles represents the hard ball. The one who keeps them relaxed and at the same time pushes down with his loin to follow the movement of the horse's back as it drops will be able to maintain contact and will not bounce.

stirrups with his knees straight, his crotch over the pommel, and his buttocks high. He should simply put enough weight on his stirrups so that his buttocks are raised very slightly and are pushed back, while his body inclines slightly forward from the hips. The head must be up and the eyes looking straight ahead, and there should be no tension in the rider's body. If he has to make an effort either to take this position or to maintain it, his legs are not placed correctly. This position has several names. Brigadier General Harry D. Chamberlain called it "the balanced position." It is also known as the "half-seat" and the "two-point seat."

The pupil must now become proficient at taking and maintaining this position at all gaits. At the posting trot it is easiest if the rider simply maintains the "up" position of the post (which should always be identical with the position we have described) rather than trying to get into it from the "down" position. He may even start by taking the position at the walk and then putting the horse into the trot before he sinks down again.

When the correct leg position is so thoroughly ingrained that the rider takes and maintains it without thinking, and when he has learned to sit without stirrups with a relaxed leg at all gaits, he can then be taught to maintain the fixed leg at the sitting trot both bareback and in the saddle without stirrups.

UPPER BODY POSITION

We have discussed in detail the position of the lower body and the legs and feet with the emphasis on relaxation. Let us now consider the upper body. To attain the correct position the mounted rider raises both hands straight up over his head, reaching for the stars and stretching his spine. His head should be up and his chin should not be pushed forward or drawn in but held in a normal position. Keeping this erect position, the rider next brings his arms down to his sides with the palms out, relaxing his shoulders but not allowing them to slouch. After doing this once or twice, he brings his arms down to shoulder height and puts his fingertips on his shoulders, palms down. From this position he brings them forward, dropping the hands to about six inches above the pommel of the saddle, keeping his wrists in position

Rider with fingertips on shoulders, and with arms lowered and hands in position to hold reins.

and rounding them slightly as though he were hugging a small keg. The hands should be sufficiently separated so that, when picking up the reins, the reins do not touch the sides of the horse's neck. The elbows will be in front of the hips, and the line running from the elbows along the forearms and reins to the horse's bit should be absolutely straight, both as seen from the side and from above. This ensures that there is no interruption of communication between the rider's hands and the horse's mouth. If the rider's elbows and wrists are kept passive except when he is using the rein aids actively, he will be able to follow the movements of the horse's head and thus keep a light tension at all times.

THE RIDER'S HANDS

There is an old saying to the effect that any man can learn to sit tight on a horse, but that God gave him his hands. It is true to the extent that certain people are blessed with a type of sensitivity that others do not have and therefore have naturally "better" hands. However, there is much that can be done to help those who have difficulty in developing the necessary skill and sensitivity.

The first thing that the rider must learn is that his hands are never to be used to keep himself in the saddle, either by using his reins as lifelines or by holding onto the saddle. To do the former disturbs and punishes the horse. To do the latter breaks the communication and gives the horse complete control. Since "grabbing leather" by an insecure rider is usually caused by a horse shying from fear or bucking from vice, the rider who has lost contact with his horse's mouth and has hence lost control will usually find himself on a terrified runaway or sitting on the ground.

The exception to the rule above is when, in learning to jump and before a secure seat has been attained, a stirrup leather is put around the horse's neck. As the horse leaves the ground the rider reaches forward and tucks a finger under it on each side to steady himself and to prevent being "left behind." When the latter occurs without a strap it results in a severe jolt on the horse's back and a hard jab on his tender bars. Too much of this will

The very young rider demonstrates the straight line which runs from the rider's elbow along his forearm and down the rein to the horse's bit.

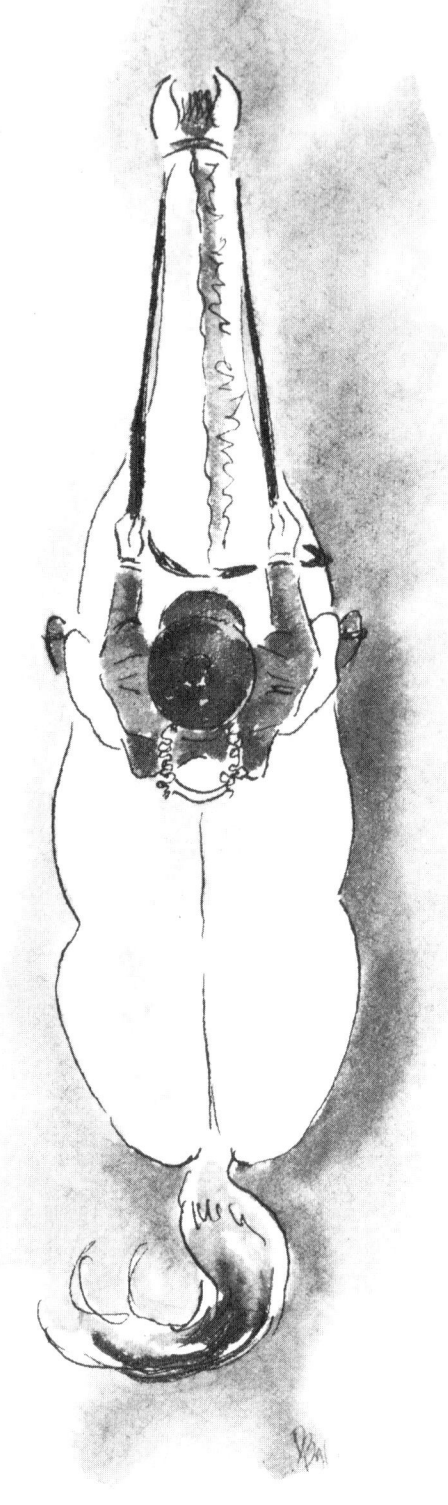

The straight line as seen from above.

make any horse reluctant to continue jumping. The expert rider will later learn to keep his reins away from the horse's neck and to follow the movements of the animal's head during the approach, take-off, flight, and landing so that the light, even tension never varies. This is extremely difficult and necessitates an absolutely independent and secure seat.

Few riders understand the extreme sensitivity of the horse's mouth. It can best be demonstrated by having the instructor place himself midway between the horse's head and his shoulder. The rider takes up his reins in the usual way and the instructor, takes a rein in each hand by reaching under the animal's neck. He asks the rider to imagine that he is the horse and to notice that when the instructor squeezes very lightly on the edges of the reins it can be clearly felt by the rider. He next imitates the movement of the horse's head at the walk, moving it forward and backward and asks the rider to see if he can follow this movement by allowing his hands to be pulled forward when necessary and bringing them back in position. Not doing so will cause the reins to flap and lose contact with the horse's mouth.

The skill required to do this takes many hours of practice before it becomes automatic, but when the rider's attention has been drawn to it, and if he is conscientious, he can work at it continuously at the walk and the canter.

At the posting trot the horse holds his head steady but the rider must learn not to raise and lower his hands as he raises and lowers his body in rising to the trot. This is best learned by extending the little fingers and touching the tips of them to the horse's withers. The goal is to keep them there as the rider posts without allowing them to bounce up and down. He can practice this first at the walk, posting as though he were trotting. It should be explained again that if the rider does not keep his hand steady the horse feels it and the communication between horse and horseman becomes garbled because the little pulls that the horse feels interrupt the contact and mislead him.

LEARNING TO INTERPRET

When the rider has reached the stage of complete control over his own body he will readily develop the second skill, that of

This picture demonstrates the epitome of the problem horseman from the horse's point of view. And the horse is taking full advantage of the fact. Starting by shying at his own shadow the horse, feeling the insecure seat, the loose reins, the wild clinging of the legs, and the banging of the heels has taken off and the rider will be lucky if he gets no more than a fall that knocks his wind out. The initial mistake was in his attempt to ride a horse of this sensitivity and caliber before he had acquired the ability to feel, to interpret, and to control his mount.

learning to interpret through the movements he feels through his seat, legs, and reins. "Horse language" is like a dialogue between two people. And unless both understand the language thoroughly there will be no successful communication. Just as the horse must learn what the rider wants him to do through signals given by his aids (legs, seat, hands, distribution of weight, and/or voice) so too the rider must learn the horse's "language" transmitted by his ears, his muscles, the changes of cadence in his gait, etc. The sensitive rider feels at once any tensing of the muscles of neck, poll, or jaw which mean that the horse is afraid or that he is about to disobey. The horse's ears tell the rider when the horse is listening to him, when he is more interested in something else, and when he is annoyed. This communication between horse and rider is continuous, the horse and rider understanding each other automatically, without thought, when all is going well. Even when the rider has received a signal that the horse is about to do something other than whatever is required, his correcting aids will be automatic and he will not have to think about what he should do to reassure the horse or prevent a disobedience.

LEARNING TO INFLUENCE

This begins with the first lesson and continues throughout the rider's career as an equestrian. He learns from every horse he rides and from every movement that he learns. An experienced horseman, mounting a strange horse for the first time, spends fifteen or more minutes at the walk and sitting trot studying the language of this particular horse. Only when he has evaluated the horse's sensitivity, his basic training, and his weaknesses does he go on to other work at the canter or over obstacles.

The inexperienced rider should imitate this practice every time he gets on a horse. He should also assign himself a series of projects, realizing that he will not be able to execute any of them perfectly, or even adequately, until he has practiced for many, many hours.

The first project is to learn to start and stop smoothly, and he should work until the merest squeeze on the reins and a slight tensing of the leg muscles will halt his horse from the walk without letting him fall over his forehand or leave his back legs spraddling. The horse should then stand a few seconds on the bit and the rider should be able to move him out equally smoothly. Learning to change from a walk to a sitting trot and back again with only the least effort on both his and the horse's part comes next. With this can go the practice of trotting an exact number of steps (say 10) followed by an equal number of steps at the walk, and repeating this again and again. Later the same exercise is done at the posting trot. When the sequence includes the canter, it should be walk, sitting trot, canter, sitting trot, walk until an exact number of steps at each gait can be demanded. Later the posting trot can be included, inserting it between sitting trot and canter.

When all of this has been learned, the rider can begin to demand the halt from the sitting trot with no intervening walking steps and the return to the trot in the same manner. This is difficult and must be absolutely smooth, and a great many horses are not so trained.

Most horses are trained to take the canter from the walk and some to take it from the halt. In teaching the horse to return to the halt or walk form the canter with no trotting steps, the emphasis must be on smoothness. There must be no break in the cadence and no hint of the "sliding stop" of the Western-trained horse. It should be like a soldier marking time who simply stops moving his feet without changing rhythm.

Causing the horse to lengthen or shorten his stride without breaking it is another fine exercise for improving the communication between horse and rider and teaching the rider the three skills of learning to feel, interpret, and influence. Riding in formation with other riders where the horses must be kept in exact relation to those beside, in front of, or behind them requires considerable skill. Simple schooling exercises such as circles, volts, and turns improve the horse physically, make him more obedient, balance him, and develop the rider's ability to communicate successfully with his mount.

The serious horseman, by remembering his goal of becoming one with his horse and by striving to improve by practice and by riding many different horses, will reap the benefit of his hours of study in an interest and sense of accomplishment a hundredfold greater than that of the happy-go-lucky rider who is content if he can walk, trot, and canter without falling off.

Furthermore, he will discover that few, if any, of the horses he rides present problems with which he cannot cope and, from the horse's point of view, he will cease to be a "problem horseman."

Index

Aggression, 18
  defensive, 22, 23
  toward other horses, 29, 30, 31
Aids, language of, 139 (*See also* hands, legs, use of back.)
Approach, to jump, *68*

Back, use of, 44
Balance, position, 125, *133*
Balance seat, 132, *133*
Balky horse, 89
Barn-rat, 84
Bending
  into corner, *63*
  lateral, *52, 53*
  neck, 44
  poll, *40*
Bit
  above the, 98
  behind the, 40
  introduction to, 104, 105
Biting, 26, 97, 107, *27*
Bits and bitting, 97–105
Bolting, 82, *85, 87*
Boring, 40, 105
Bridling, headshy horse, 15, *17*
Bucking, 90

Cadence of gaits, 47
Canter, 50
Catching the horse in the field, 118, 119
Charging, 28
Check-reins, 40, *41*
Centaur, 123, *124*
Clipping, 111
Confidence of horse in rider, 38
Confusion, 9, 37, 62, *8*
Counter-change of hands, 50, *57*
Cribbing, 106
Crowding
  the rider, 90
  in the stall, 105, *107*

Direction, change of, 51, 82, *70*

Dressage and training figures, 50, 51, *52, 53, 54, 55, 56, 57*

Eohippus, 6
Exercise, lack of, 10
Exercises, *see* Dressage figures, equitation, 50

Fear, 6, *7, 13*
  of the bit, 38, *39*
  of specific objects, 7, 8, *7*
  of spurs, 67
  of stepping on strange objects or footing, 79, *81*
  of traffic, 80, 82
Feel, learning to, 123, 125
Figures, *see* Dressage simple, 46
Flexing, of the poll, 40, *43*
Foot, lifting of, 12, *13*

Goal, of the horseman, 123, *125*
Goals, training, 77
Grain, effect of, 10

Hackamore, 40, 44, 51, 103, 105, *42*
Half-pass (two-track), 50, *56, 57*
Half-seat, 132
Half-turn, 76, *66*
Halter-breaking, 109, *110,* 113
Halting, 44
Handling
  aggressive horse, 26, *27*
  biters, 26, *27*
  headshy horse, 15, *17*
  kickers and kicking, 28, 91, *92*
Hands, 134, 137, *132, 135, 136*
Head
  position of, 98, *100, 101*
  tossing of, 98
Headshyness, 15, *17*
Herdbound, 84, 86, 109, *87, 89*
High spirits, 10
Horse, as instructor, 122, 139
Horseman
  experienced, 125

problem, 120, 121
Horseman's goal, 123, 140, *125*

Influence, learning to, 139–141
Interpret, learning to, 123, 137–139

Jump, bad approach to, *68*
Jumper
  prevention of abuse of, 73
  reschooling, 67–73, *68*
  training of, 67–73, *74*
Jumping
  cross-country, 72
  in company, 72
Jumping equipment, for beginners, 73, *74*
Jumps, mental hazard, 76

Kickers, 26, 28, 29
Kicking
  at other horses, 29
  cow-kicking, 92
  in the stable, 106, *108*

Leading, 77–79, 109, *81, 110*
Legs
  fixed, 130
  position of rider's, 126, 130
  swinging, 127, *131*
Leg-yield, 50, *54, 55*
Loading, 114, *115, 116, 117*

Measuring length of stride, 47, *45*
Medication, controlling the nervous horse for, 118
Mounting the restless horse, 91, 94, 95, *92, 93, 96, 97*
Mental-hazard jumps, 76

Nervous horse, *see* timidity, fear

One-sided horse, 50
Overhead, check rein, 40, *41*

Poll
  flexing of, 40
  stiffening of, 40, *39, 100, 101*
Position, balance, 131, 132, *133*
Posting trot, 130, 132, *131*
Pulley rein, 82, 84, *85, 87*

Race horse, re-schooling of for hacking or jumping
  brush-racer and steeplechaser, 73
  standardbred, 73
  thoroughbred (flat racer), 73
Rearing, 86, 89
Rein-back, 34, 40
Renvers, 51, *60, 61*
Resistance, 62
Restlessness while being mounted, 91, 94, 95, *92, 93, 96, 97*
Rider, problem, 121, *138*
Rolling in the saddle, 98
Re-schooling
  race horse, 75, 76
  timid horse, 12

Seat, 125, 126, 133, *129*
  balance, 132, 133
  two-point, 132
  half-seat, 132
Sensitive horse, 38
Sensitivity, of mouth of horse, 137
Shoulder-in, 50, *52, 53*
Shying, 78
Side-reins, 51, *64*
Sitting-bones, 126
Skills, basic, 73
Stable problems, 105, 106
Stall-courage, 95
Stallions, 19 to 25, *21, 23*
Star-gazing, 40, 105
Stiffness
  in the poll, 40, 43, *39*
  lateral, 50
Stride, measuring of, 47, *45*
Stubbornness, 31, 34, 82, *9, 35, 83*
Sulkiness, 31, *35, 9*

Timid horse, 11, 12
Timid rider, 122
Tossing the head, 98
Training
  foal to follow, 67, *81*
  on roads and trails, 80
  re-schooling the race horse, 75
  timid horse, 11
Training goals, 77
Training hunters and jumpers, 67–73, *68, 74*
Training methods
  bad, 62

Transitions
　of gaits, 34
　hackmore to snaffle, 51
Travers, *58, 59*
Trot
　posting, 130, 132, *131*
　sitting, 46, 120, *127, 128, 129*
　strong, 46, 47, *32, 33*
Turning, in jumping, 70, *71*
　to correct bolting, 82, *85, 87*
Twitch, 14, *16*

Two-point seat, 132, *133*
Two-track (half-pass), 50, *56*
　counter-change of hands at the, 50, *57*

Upper body position, 132, 133

Vanning, 114, *81, 115, 116, 117*

Walk, 45, 46, *48, 49*